THE SMART MEMORY COURSE

THE QUICKSTART GUIDE TO MEMORY IMPROVEMENT, SKILLS AND THEORY

BEN CUNNINGHAM

Foreword

Memory is one of the most powerful assets a human being has at their disposal. As we age, memory can fade, but there are tools and exercises at hand to help retain our memory long into old age. This does not mean that one's memory should be neglected and that improvement can wait, the exercises within this book will help keep your memory at its optimum and starting early is the best way to maintain a powerful memory long into the future.

The SMART Memory Course has been written with the modern day professional at mind. In today's busy and often hectic lifestyles memory improvement and memory maintenance often fall at the bottom of the list. People often do not realise that a better memory is the secret to unlock a more productive lifestyle.

Without a doubt strong memory skills can help you achieve more in your day to day lives, but what is sometimes more important are the memories you make. You are making good memories everyday, ensure that these are not lost.

- Helen Christensen, MD

CONTENTS

Introduction

Are you forgetful?

Do you often fail to remember small details? Do you walk into a room and forget what you went in there for? Do you find information is often on the "tip of your tongue"?

Many things can affect whether or not you retain information. This can include a stressful period in your life, how many things you're actually trying to remember, and whether or not you're actually paying attention when the information is given to you. The list goes on.

However, did you know that it's entirely possible to actually train your brain to remember things more effectively?

By understanding how the brain works, how it retains information, where and why, you'll start to have a much deeper understanding of the organ that we all rely upon completely. Within that, you can also learn techniques to retain that information, allowing you to become a memory master in no time!

By picking up this book you've shown an intention to do just that.

The Smart Memory Course is going to take you on a journey from the current state of play to something much more impressive!

You can improve your memory, you can remember those things you always find yourself forgetting, and by doing all of this, you'll become a much more productive person overall.

No more forgetting important tasks at work, no more walking into a room to do something only to forget what it was when you get there, and no more "it's on the tip of my tongue" moments.

High quality memory retention is yours if you put in the effort and work on the techniques we talk about throughout this book.

WHY IS MEMORY IMPORTANT?

It might sound like a ridiculous question, but let's just dwell on it for a second.

As we age, it's normal to become a little forgetful. The brain ages just as the rest of the body does, and that means that the occasional piece of information slips between the gaps. In some cases, the situation can worsen, leading to degenerative conditions such as dementia and Alzheimer's.

However, studies have shown that by working your brain harder, by challenging your own mind and using exercises to keep it fit and healthy, you can actually maintain your brain and memory bank for much longer.

Why leave it until you're heading into old age? Why not start now?

The benefits are pretty impressive when you delve a little deeper.

We all need a quality memory to get through the day. Sure, you can forget the odd detail and get away with it; in some ways, a little forgetfulness is endearing, but when it becomes a chronic habit, it can quickly turn from endearing to infuriating in an instant!

In a work situation, having a good memory is key.

If you can remember small details, you're not going to miss deadlines and targets, and you're going to be far more productive as a result. On a personal note, isn't it nice to think that you're going to remember the small details and memories for many years to come? Working out your memory and making it stronger and more effective will do just that.

Think of your memory like a muscle. When you go to the gym to work on your abs or your biceps, you use strength training to make it strong. You flex those muscles and make them work, you sweat a little and in the end, you see bulk forming, definition, and the results are clear for all to see. Improving your memory is a little like going to the gym for brains!

The more you work that brain of yours, and the more you do it in the right way, the stronger it will become.

There are countless exercises you can use to improve memory recall, but some are more effective than others. Throughout the Smart Memory Course, we're going to focus on results. We're going to talk you through the best exercises there are for memory improvement and we're going to demonstrate how easy they are to do, provided you're happy to put in the time and effort in order to notice results.

It won't happen overnight, that's something you need to bear in mind, but results will come if you work hard enough.

It's almost like a snowball effect in many ways; at first nothing seems to be happening, but then slowly you start to notice small effects occurring, and then suddenly it's like an avalanche! As the snowball rolls down the hill it picks up momentum until it's an unstoppable force. Think of your memory a little like that, only less cold and wet!

THE BRAIN IS A COMPLEX THING

It might be small, it might not weigh very much, and to be honest, it's pretty ugly, but the brain is a highly complex and sophisticated organ that lives inside your skull. Yes, as you're reading this, your brain is the human computer which is deciphering these squiggles into letters, forming words, sounds, and making sense of it all, literally within less than a split second.

No other computer on the planet can ever hope be as sophisticated as your brain, and so much of it is still not completely understood. What we do know however, is that the short term and long term memory bank that lives within your brain can be altered with a little training.

Think of it like rewiring an old radio or TV and upgrading it to something more in the moment. That's what we're going to do to your brain!

So, make yourself comfortable, grab a cup of coffee, and if you really need to, a pen and paper for making notes. First we're going to talk about the brain and how it retains memories, to give you the background information you need for further understanding, before we finally get onto the practical elements, the exercises which will allow you to flex those brain muscles, rewire the old model into something new and HD, and therefore upgrade your memory for the coming years.

Let's begin!

Chapter 1: Memory 101

Let's get started!

In order to improve your own memory, you first need to understand what the memory is.

The chapter is going to give you the basic lowdown on the brain in terms of memory storage, how the memory stores information, how it recalls information, and how your senses tie into it all.

You might wonder why we're delving into biology right now, but you can't fully understand something unless you know how it works. If you seriously want to improve your memory, you need to know about it on a deeper level. Consider this chapter your quick go-to guide for everything memory-related. By the end of it, you're not going to be a neurologist, but you'll have a grasp on what the brain does and how it remember things at least.

Brain Anatomy - Memories

We can't talk about what the brain does in its entirety. Firstly, the word count won't cover it and secondly, even the most experienced scientists still have questions about how the brain works completely.

The good news is scientists have long been trying to study the memory and as a result, we've got quite a few answers on what exactly is going on in there.

At first, scientists thought the entire brain played a part in memory storage and recollection, but then they delved a little deeper and found that there are four specific parts of the brain which are mainly associated with the memory, with neurotransmitters playing a vital part too. These sections of the brain are:

- Amygdala
- Hippocampus
- Cerebellum
- Prefrontal cortex

In order to understand how memories are formed, where they're stored and how they're recalled, we really need to learn more about these key parts of the brain.

AMYGDALA

When you attempt to learn anything about the brain, one specific term you'll see popping up time and time again is 'amygdala'. This is a small part of the brain which is located on the temporal lobe, close to the hippocampus, another part of the brain heavily associated with memories.

The amygdala allows you to feel emotions, and it is thought that some people have a more active or sensitive amygdala than others. For instance, if you're someone who really feels emotions quite keenly, you have a sensitive amygdala, as this part of the brain is designed to regulate emotions. The same can be said for anyone who has a high degree of empathy; the amygdala is the part of the brain which allows you to understand and appreciate the emotions of other people, allowing you to handle situations in different ways.

In terms of memory formation and recollection, the amygdala plays an emotional role here still. Any memory which is linked to fear or worry is connected to the amygdala. These types of memories are formed here because of the stress reaction which occurs when we experience the 'flight or flight response'.

Back in the days of the cave people, whenever a predator appeared, or something which was a real cause for worry, the fight or flight response saved lives, signaling them to either run and hide, or fight. Our lives have developed since then thankfully, but our stress response hasn't. This means our brain, thanks to the amygdala, still looks for threats and floods our bodies with endorphins and hormones to cope with the oncoming fight or the need to run. The problem is, it often misinterprets what a threat really is, and that's when too much stress can become a problem.

In terms of memory formation, the stress hormones which are released during this fight or flight response, namely cortisol, help a particular memory of a threat become burned into your memory bank. It's almost a defense mechanism; your memory will hold that particular thought and will quickly bring it back if it senses that the past is about to repeat itself, giving you a quick head's up to either run and hide, or get ready to fight what is coming.

So, you might hear a specific noise and suddenly freeze. That is your amygdala kicking into action and recognizing a threat from the past. Neurotransmitters in and around the amygdala suddenly fire up and give you a head's up about something which caused you upset or trouble in the past.

In addition to storing and remembering troublesome memories such as this, the amygdala is also known to help transfer memories from the short-term memory to the long-term memory, if they have a particular emotional connection. In our next chapter we're going to talk more about the types of memories you have and where they're stored, but it's worth noting that the short term memory holds information which you are going literally forget in an hour; these are deemed to be useless pieces of information which your long term memory doesn't need. Long term memories however are held for long periods of time, often a full lifetime.

For now, you simply need to know that anything related to an emotional memory will have been recognized and stored by the amygdala.

HIPPOCAMPUS

The next part of the brain which plays a strong part in memory formation and storage is the hippocampus. Located close to the amygdala, shaped like a seahorse and a vital part of the limbic system, the hippocampus plays an extremely part in consolidating information and deciding whether it remains in the short term memory bank or whether it is transferred for longer term storage. The hippocampus also retrieves memories and presents them to you.

Whilst the amygdala is linked to emotional memories, the hippocampus is mostly linked to spatial memories, e.g. when you are asked to recall something factual. This could be finding your way out of a maze, for example, or remembering how something tasted.

The hippocampus also ensures that memories have a meaning, so when you recall them they make sense to you and aren't just a jumbled mess of noises and sounds. It also connects memories to one another. For instance, have you ever remembered something and then it's led you on to remember something which happened associated with it? That work is done by the hippocampus.

If you unfortunately develop damage in the hippocampus area, perhaps via a car accident or general blow to the head, you'll likely to have trouble remembering things from that point on. It's possible that you would remember things from the past, e.g.

memories which had already been transferred into your long term memory, but you would have severe trouble forming new memories, and you may even notice that your long term memories are a little disorientated.

We're going to talk bout how memories are recalled a little later in the chapter, and you'll learn more about the vital work of the hippocampus then.

CEREBELLUM & PREFRONTAL CORTEX

We will link these two parts together as they work hand in hand and are located very close to one another.

We know that the hippocampus is key for processing memories, and that if you sustain an injury to that part of your brain you would have problems with your memory from that point on, but the cerebellum and the prefrontal cortex also play a very key role too.

The cerebellum is responsible for controlling and remembering how to move. For instance, this part of the brain allows you to move your arms, your legs, how to chew etc. It is located right at the very back of your skull. On the other hand, the prefrontal cortex holds the information on sensory reactions. So, these two parts of the brain work together to help you move and feel, processing the information required to do these things.

But, how does that link in to memory?

Both the cerebellum and the prefrontal cortex are known to help transfer information to your short term memory bank, as well as helping you to make strong decisions.

Whilst these two parts of the brain might not have the same strong part to play as the amygdala and the hippocampus, they do a task which completes the circle.

WHERE ARE MEMORIES ACTUALLY STORED?

Now you know the parts of the brain which play a part in storing and forming memories, where are they actually kept?

There is no secret filing cabinet in your brain which opens and closes whenever a new memory is committed to it and an old one dragged out. Memories are stored and decoded in various different places around the brain, but the main piece of anatomy which is closest to being that magical memory filing cabinet is the hippocampus once more.

Again, we'll touch upon the types of memories you have in our next chapter and that will shed some more light on where they're actually kept but in terms of episodic memories, i.e. memories which are autobiographical, the hippocampus is where you'll find them.

So, if you had a coffee yesterday and you remember the taste of it, your hippocampus is firing up its neurotransmitters to help you remember it. Then, you'll start to remember the smell as well as the taste. Again, this is your neurotransmitters pulling the memory out and the associated meaning which was attached to it when the memory was committed to your memory bank, coming to the fore.

Again, it's all down to the hippocampus.

What Happens When You're Remembering Something?

If you're still a little confused by this point, don't worry, that's totally normal.

Scientists have been studying the human brain for years, decades even, and they're still not completely sure about it either, so you're not going to be sure after half a chapter! What you need to know however is that various parts of the brain all link together to form connections, which allows memories to be stored and recalled.

The point of this chapter isn't to make you a brain specialist, and if you find that you're deeply interested in brain anatomy after reading this chapter, it's a great idea to go on and do some further reading. It's certainly a fascinating subject, albeit a complicated one.

In terms of improving your own memory however, it's simply about having a basic understanding of where memories are stored and how. That's all you really need to know.

When you learn something new, perhaps a room number or someone's name you've known for ten seconds, that information is retained quickly in your short term memory. The hippocampus then decides what to do with that information. It pulls your senses together to create one full memory, rather than several different small ones. So, if you were at a restaurant and you enjoyed a meal, you will remember the whole meal, including the way it smelled, tasted and looked, and not three different memories covering each sense.

The connections between different neurons around the brain are also responsible for helping you to remember things which are connected to the original memory. So if you think back to the restaurant with the delicious meal we just mentioned, you might also then suddenly remember that it was raining that night and you had worn a red top.

So, what happens when you suddenly remember something?

How does it all come together?

If you were to have a scan of your brain during memory recollection, the picture would show various different parts of your brain sparking into action; this would show as a light picture. As a result, different parts of your brain are pulling information out of the memory bank and quickly linking them together to recall the one picture. This is all collected and decoded in the hippocampus once more, which presents the full memory to you.

Our brains have the capacity for infinite memories, but most of the time we struggle to remember small pieces of information that we use on a regular basis. Why is that?

Forgetting something can come down to many different reasons. It could be that the brain is degenerating, i.e. in old age, and as a result the connection between memories aren't as clear, the memory wasn't properly transferred to the long term memory bank in the first place, you're feeling stressed and can't concentrate, or that you are intentionally trying to forget it, and it's interfering with memory recall.

Studies into memory recollection, storage, and everything else to do with this very broad ranging subject are ongoing and will probably remain that way for decades still.

Points to Remember From This Chapter

In this chapter we've introduced the basics of brain anatomy related to memory and we've covered information on how senses are drawn into the picture. It's a lot of information to take on board if you want to really understand the brain, but the basics are usually enough to allow you to concentrate on improving your memory.

As we move through the various practical elements a little later in the book, you'll come to see why basic brain anatomy is a useful thing to learn about.

In this first chapter, the main points to bear in mind are:

•	Memories are stored in various places within the brain, but the hippocampus is the most important structure in terms of committing pictures and experiences to the short and long term memories banks and retrieving them in a full memory picture
•	The amygdala plays a part in memory recollection and storage, provided there is a strong emotion connected to that particular memory
•	The cerebellum and prefrontal cortex are also associated with memory storage and recollection
•	There is no specific part of the brain where memories are held, but various structures which work together to retrieve them
•	If you damage your hippocampus, you are likely to have

problems with your memory from that point onwards

•   Neurotransmitters fire up when a memory is being stored or recalled, helping to transmit information from place to place

•   Senses work hand in hand with the hippocampus, allowing you to remember how something smelled, tasted, felt, and looked

•   You are not expected to know everything about the brain, but having basic knowledge is useful!

Chapter 2: Types of Memories

In our first chapter we covered the various different parts of the brain which are linked with memory formation, storage, and recollection, but now we need to talk about the different types of memories we hold.

Some memories we know we're retaining, others are committed to our memory banks without us even realizing. Then, a few years later we suddenly remember something and it seems so random that we can't explain it! That is because we have conscious and subconscious memories. These fall into various subtypes.

Overall, there are three main memory types:

- The sensory memory
- Short term memory
- Long term memory

Within each of these categories are other types of memories which are stored there. Let's explore each one in turn.

THE SENSORY MEMORY

If we rated these memory types in terms of time spent, the sensory memory would hold information for the shortest time. These are things you remember for a few seconds and then suddenly forget. They flash into your mind and then boom! They're gone again.

Memories which are processed via the sensory memory are lights, sounds, feels, tastes, linking in to each of our five senses. There are several different subtypes of sensory memory, including:

•	Iconic memory - A quick flash which you remember very fleetingly, e.g. an error message which flashes up on your computer screen and then disappears. These typically last for half a second at the most.

•	Echoic memory - This type of memory is a sound memory and they're remembered for no more than four seconds at the most. You might hear a song on the radio and you'll sing the tune back and then forget it. That is an echoic memory.

•	Haptic memory - This type of memory relates to touch. You might feel the roughness of a rock and then a few seconds later you forget about it.

Short Term Memory

Anything which lasts more than four seconds at most (an echoic memory) is committed to your short term memory and decoded there. It may make it to your long term memory, but it's far more likely that you will forget it after a few minutes at the most.

However, if you think to yourself "I need to remember to buy milk" just before you go to the supermarket, it is your short term memory which will allow you to remember to buy that milk, and then forget about it forever.

A good way to try and extend the amount of time you keep a piece of information in your short term memory is to repeat it over and over again until you don't need it anymore. For instance, if someone tells you a telephone number and you're running to get your phone to input it, chant the number over and over until you input it and then you'll instantly forget it afterwards.

Long Term Memory

The long term memory, as the name suggests, stores all the memories you have from days gone by. It is an extremely complex and hard to understand system, which even scientists haven't quite got to grips with just yet!

Long term memories can range from something which happened in your life ten minutes ago, to something which happened in your childhood. We mentioned conscious and subconscious memories at the beginning of this chapter and the long term memory holds both types.

Conscious memories require us to try and focus on the memory to bring more details to the fore, whilst unconscious memories appear in our mind without much effort, e.g. remembering how to drive to your family home.

As with sensory memories, there are several types of long term memories too.

•   Explicit memories - These are conscious memories and when you remember things, it's because you mean to. You focus on the memory and try and pull it to the front of your mind. It could be remembering your address, remembering your driving license number, basically anything that you know is in your memory bank but you have to focus to bring it forward.

•   Declarative memories - These types of memories are pieces of information that you know you need to remember for a specific point in time, e.g. a friend's birthday. You will then know that when July, or whenever you friends birth is, you'll remember the date and know to buy a present.

•   Episodic memories - These memories are events and experiences you have had throughout your life. For instance, it could be a meal you had at a local restaurant which you want to tell your friend about, or someone asks you what you did last night and you have to think back and remember. These are episodic memories because they are events or experiences.

• Semantic memories - These are facts, data, and pieces of knowledge which you store away in your memory for a later date. For instance, it could be remembering the name of your dentist, or your friend asks you what the name of the guy from that TV show is. A semantic memory will give you that information.

• Implicit memories - Have you ever had a hunch about something, e.g. "oh that rings a bell"? In that case you're trying to recall an implicit memory. These are often unconscious memories because you don't recall specific details. A good example of this is something you experienced in your childhood, e.g. you went somewhere and then when you go back a few years later you suddenly remember.

• Procedural memories - This is when you know how to do something, e.g. you know how to type on a keyboard, drive a car, or ride a bike.

• Auditory memories - This is predictably about noises and sounds. Children use auditory memories to help them to learn how to read, speak and play instruments. When teaching a child how to read, teachers are taught about how auditory memories are formed themselves. You would say the letter 'D' and show the child the written letter at the same time. By doing that, you're helping them to form an auditory memory in their long term memory.

• Visual-spatial memories - Finally, we have visual-spatial memories. This is when you are shown a picture of something and you put a label to it. So, if a child was learning about farm yard animals, you would show them a picture of a cow and say the word "cow". They then associate the picture with the word and when they see cow in real life they know what it's called.

Again, the point of this chapter is to give you information and help you understand the scope of the types of memories your brain is capable of holding. Some memories don't remain in your mind, and some stay there for the rest of your days.

Points to Remember From This Chapter

From our first chapter we know that the hippocampus plays a very key role in decoding memories and deciding where they go, but now you also know about the different types of memories that we all have. Guaranteed, you have one of every type of memory in your brain, in fact you probably have many, many more than one!

It's fascinating to learn about what our brains are actually capable of.

The main points to bear in mind from this chapter are:

• We have three main types of memory banks - the sensory memory, the short term memory, and the long term memory

• Sensory memories are typically retained for no more than a few seconds at the very most and are always associated with a type of sense, such as touch, smell, visual sparks or lights, etc

• The short term memory can hold information for a few minutes before it is forgotten

• You can extend the amount of time a piece of information stays in your short term memory by chanting it over and over, until you no longer need it

•	The long term memory can hold information you learnt from five minutes previously, and will stay there for the rest of your days. You might find it harder to remember memories from your long term memory bank as time goes on, but they will be in there somewhere!

•	There are various different types of long term memories, which are defined by the way the memory was formed or what it is about, almost like a filing cabinet in your brain.

Chapter 3: Easy Daily Memory Improvement Exercises to Try

Now it's time to get practical.

We know what the memory is and what it comprises of, and we also know that scientists have had a pretty hard time trying to come up with concrete explanations. There's no time to dwell on that however; if you want to improve your memory, you have to put unanswered questions aside and focus on techniques which will help you achieve your aims.

A little later in the book we're going to cover specific in-depth techniques which will rewire your brain in some ways and make your memory stronger. However, you also need to use daily exercises which are quick and simple. These exercise won't bring you instant results, but they will stretch your memory muscles to allow them to become stronger over time.

The more you practice these techniques, the more effective they will become, the easier they'll become, and the more benefit you'll notice.

The three techniques we're going to cover are:

- The Sound Alike Method
- Rhymes and Jingles
- Mind Maps

If you do your own research, you might identify some other techniques that you might like to try, but these four are known to be some of the most effective overall. For that reason, we'll focus on these for better results.

Let's go!

THE SOUND ALIKE METHOD

A very quick and easy way to remember a piece of information that you really don't want to forget is to come up with a word or phrase that the piece of information sounds like.

For example, if you want to remember someone's name, such as Greg, you would try and think of a word which sounds like 'Greg'. So you could say Peg. In order to attach the sound alike to the name, you also need to use a little visualization.

Try this:

•   Say the word aloud which you want to remember, in this case it would be the name 'Greg'

•   Visualize Greg's face in your mind

•   Identify the word which you're going to use to remember his name, but make sure it's a word that means something to you, or a word you use a lot. In this case, let's assume you do a lot of washing and you're going to use the word 'peg'. You're going to use this because it rhymes, i.e. 'sounds alike', so Greg rhymes with peg

•   Then, visualize Greg's face in your mind and attach the peg to him. Keep the picture in your mind and repeat the words 'Greg' and 'peg'

•   Make sure the rhyme is clear in your mind before you move on from your visualization

When you're trying to remember someone's name, it's likely that their face is going to pop into your mind before their name does. That's why we often hear the phrase "it's on the tip of my tongue'; basically you can see what you want to remember but the words evade you.

So, when Greg's face pops into your mind, the image you've used with the peg attached to him will remind you of the word 'peg'. The sound alike attachment you've made between 'Greg' and 'peg' will help you remember his name.

The more outrageous or crazy a visual you can put onto this type of memory trigger the better. The reason is, the weirder the image, the more likely you are to remember it! So, in this case you could picture Greg with the peg stuck on his nose, or a huge peg stuck to the top of his head. You'll be able to recall the image far easier if it's unusual.

It doesn't have to be names you use, it can be for any specific piece of information you're trying to remember. The word doesn't have to rhyme either, it simply needs to sound like it, or have a very close association with it, and something you're sure to remember. Adding in the visual element gives you an extra push towards recalling the piece of information, because the image is likely to trigger the memory.

Rhymes And Jingles

Another very common way of remembering information, and one which is a little similar to the previous example, is to use different rhymes and jingles.

If you think back to when you were at school, your teacher probably taught you songs, e.g. the alphabet song, number songs, colors of the rainbow, etc. The reason behind this is because music is extremely powerful in terms of memory triggers, just like smells are too.

You've no doubt heard a song on the radio that you've not heard for years and it's suddenly taken you back in time to the period of your life when you first heard it. For example, you might have had a favorite band in your teenage years and when you hear a song from them after many years, you're suddenly back being a teenager again for a second!

That's how powerful music can be in terms of memory triggers.

In this particular technique you're going to use the same kinds of rhymes or even jingles that your teacher used when they were trying to teach you the basics of language or numbers. Think back to the rainbow song, "red and yellow and pink and green, orange and purple and blue, I can sing a rainbow …" you're singing it now aren't you? And you're picturing a rainbow in your mind because the association of a visual and the song is triggering a piece of information in your long term memory bank.

Whilst you were learning this at school, you also repeated it constantly. The key is in repetition. The more you repeat something, the more you will commit it to your memory and the easier it will be to remember it in the future.

It's far easier to remember a song with a catchy line than it is to remember a sentence or a string of numbers, such as someone's phone number. However, if you insert those numbers into a song, you're more likely to remember them.

In mass advertising, marketers use catchy jingles in their campaigns. They're not doing his because they sound good, they're doing it because they're trying to subliminally commit the jingle to your memory and as as result, the product it is associated with will stick in there too. As a result, you're more likely to make a purchase.

To use this method for your own memory requirements, try this:

•	Think of the piece of information that you're trying to remember, be it someone's address or your phone number
•	Try and picture it in your mind as an object - is it a color? What does it look like?
•	Come up with a catchy song which encompasses the information and the way it looks in your mind. It can be anything, it can be as ridiculous as you like; in fact, the more ridiculous, the better!
•	Repeat it over and over, sing it to yourself
•	The more you repeat it, the more it will remain in your mind

Mind Maps

Our final easy daily exercise is mind mapping.

You've probably heard of mind maps before, but they're actually a very effective way to remember a lot of information in one go and rely upon forming associations between keywords and list of information which is related to it. This is a very important method in improving memory recall, as associations form strong bonds in the long term memory and aid with recall overall.

A mind map looks a lot like a brainstorming session. There is usually one word in the middle, i.e. the main theme of the idea you're trying to remember, and several other pieces of information or ideas shooting from it, exactly like a brainstorming diagram.

The plus point of a mind map is that you're able to remember a large amount of information without having to organize it into any sense. Your ideas will appear naturally, allowing you to analyze them naturally.

This particular idea is great for remember information which would otherwise be quite dull or even monotonous. You can create a diagram in your mind which is colorful and which may even include pictures. The words you include within the map are keywords, words which trigger an association or reminder of the rest of the information pertaining to it.

The more color and imagination you can put into your mind map, the more likely you are to remember it. So, go to town in the design!

Try this:

• Write down a central keyword of the item you're trying to remember. Keep it as brief and easy to remember as possible. Draw a circle around it, with color if possible and decorate it a little. The more creative your mind map, the easier you will remember it

• Now, draw your first line which shoots away from the keyword and add in another associated keyword in a bubble or cloud; again, make it creative. Keep the keywords short, but make sure they make strong sense to you and have a firm association with the information you want to remember as a whole

• Repeat the process with other pieces of information, in other 'off shoots'

• Make your final mind map as colorful as you can; again, the brighter it is, the more likely you are to recall it quickly and accurately

• Once the mind map is complete, spend some time looking at it and memorizing it. Don't expect to commit it to your memory straightaway, but keep a copy of it close to you. Whenever you look at it, you'll memorize it a little more

• The hope is that by the end, you can throw away the paper copy and keep the mental version in your memory bank.

Points to Remember From This Chapter

In this chapter we've talked about three easy memory exercises you can use on a daily basis to help you remember certain pieces of small information. As we move through the book we're going to go into more detail and learn more complex techniques, to help you remember more information over the long term, and boost your memory performance in general.

For now however, these three methods are ideal for helping you to strengthen your memory muscles. Find one which suits you, or use all three if you can find benefit in them, but it's usually better to stick to one or two, to avoid confusing yourself.

The main points to take from this chapter are:

• Daily memory exercises are useful for helping you to remember small but useful pieces of information

• Visualization and rhymes are ideal for forming strong connections and associations in your mind, and therefore allowing quicker and more effective memory recall

• The Sound a Like Method uses words which sounds like the word you're trying to remember, and then attaches an image to it. The more detailed and obscure the image, the more likely you are to remember it

• Repetition is key with every type of memory exercise - don't expect results overnight

• Music and jingles are very powerful in memory recall, with advertising campaigns using them on a regular basis

• Coming up with a song or jingle which encompasses the information important you want to remember is a good way to keep it in your mind

• Mind maps are ideal for remembering large amounts of information or ideas

• A mind map uses the art of association, which is key strong memory recall

• The more colorful and creative your mind map, the more likely you are to remember what the key words mean, giving you a full picture of recalled information.

Chapter 4: How Does Your Lifestyle Affect Your Memory?

Improving your memory isn't all about learning techniques and visualizing images and songs, it actually encompasses a large amount of smaller facets too. For instance, did you know that what you eat can affect your memory? How much you move? How much sleep you get?

These are all lifestyle issues which can either improve your memory or reduce it. Assuming that memory improvement is all about learning techniques is incorrect - you need to focus on your health and wellbeing as a huge priority if you want to be healthy on the inside and outside, both physically and mentally.

In this chapter we're going to explore the role of lifestyle in memory improvement and talk about some of the changes you can make to help you boost your memory function over the long term. Of course, you need to work with the techniques we're going to cover later in the book at the same time, but they work hand in hand - if you don't make changes to your lifestyle and rectify issues, you're wasting your time; however if you dedicate time to lifestyle changes and memory work, you're looking at a very positive outcome.

Our health and wellbeing affects every single part of our lives. When you're feeling sluggish and lacking in energy, your mood dips and you're not productive in your job. You might also find that it's harder to remember things, simply because you're in a space which isn't very positive.

On the flip side, if you're feeling energized and healthy, it's likely that you'll find it easier to recall the details you need.

There are things you need to do in terms of your lifestyle and there are things you need to stop doing. Generally speaking, if you make an effort boost your health and wellbeing, you'll find that your cognitive function will improve as a happy side effect. This includes your memory function generally.

WANT TO IMPROVE YOUR MEMORY? AVOID ALCOHOL

Whilst it's perfectly fine to have the odd drink in moderation, heavy alcohol usage could actually damage your ability to remember the small details.

Think back to the last time you had a rather grim 'morning after the night before' and you were struggling with a hangover. Could you clearly remember the details from that big night out, or were some a little hazy, or even completely blank?

That is because when you drink alcohol, you're making it harder for your brain to recognize information and transfer it to the short term memory bank and then to the long term bank. In this case, information is simply forgotten instead, acting basically as a piece of sensory memory, as we explored in our previous chapter on memory types. It's lost within seconds. That is why when you wake up the next morning and you're wracking your brain, asking yourself if you actually paid the bill or not, you can't quite remember.

If you drink heavily over the long-term, it's entirely possible to damage your memory completely. In this case, the hippocampus, the piece of the brain which is so vital in terms of memory storage and recall, can actually start to reduce in size. This means that the neurons within the hippocampus shrink down too, along with the cells. Basically, that vital piece of brain isn't as capable as before.

The same can be said for long-term drug use. By this we're talking about the types of drugs which you shouldn't be using, not the prescription drugs which you're taking as advised by your doctor. Taking illegal drugs recreationally does exactly the same as drinking heavy amounts of alcohol - it damages the memory to the point where you'll struggle to recall the small details. In some cases, this damage is irreversible.

Put simply - don't do drugs. At all.

Another reason why you may struggle with details after a heavy night on the wine is because glutamate is adversely affected by alcohol.

Glutamate is a brain chemical which can have an effect on your memory. When this chemical reacts badly to alcohol in certain amounts (this will vary from person to person) you may completely forget details. It is thought that black spots that can occur in the memory after a night of heavy drinking is down to this chemical and its reaction to alcohol.

DOES THIS MEAN YOU SHOULD NEVER DRINK ALCOHOL AGAIN?

No. It simply means that you need to drink carefully and in moderation. Avoid binge drinking, e.g. not drinking all week and then going out on a Saturday night and drinking a week's work of units. This is particularly damaging.

A glass or two of wine with a meal is not going to cause you major problems, but if you find you're repeating the process every single night, you might want to cut back a little.

Moderation is key and that means monitoring your intake and being honest with yourself.

THREE KEY LIFESTYLE CHANGES TO BOOST YOUR MEMORY

Aside from ensuring that you drink alcohol only in moderation and you avoid taking any recreational drugs, what other lifestyle changes can you make which will help boost your memory performance?

There are three main areas to focus on.

Make Sleep a Priority

It is impossible to function if you are sleep deprived, and you actually start to show signs of sleep deprivation far sooner than you might think. After 24 hours without sleep you are starting to show signs of this issue, and studies have shown that if you are awake for a solid 24 hours without sleep, your blood alcohol content starts to rise.

Basically, after 24 hours without sleep, you're showing signs that you've been drinking alcohol, even when you haven't! We've already covered the memory effects of drinking alcohol, and not getting enough sleep can do exactly the same thing.

Sleep is a priority because it allows your body the time to heal and recover from the stresses and strains you put it through on a daily basis. It's not just your body that heals and rests, but your brain too. If you're working hard every day, stressed out, and trying to juggle a million balls in the air, your brain needs to chill out for a little while! If you don't allow it the time to do so, you're going to notice effects, including in your memory.

How much sleep should you get? This varies from person to person, but the general advice is that a grown adult should be aiming between 7 to 8 hours of interrupted sleep per night. Just one night of interrupted sleep or a lack of sleep can cause you to have a sleep deficit, which could take days to recoup.

Studies have shown that adults who regularly get a solid 8 hours of sleep per night are more effective at recognizing people and details, and remembering specifics, compared those who didn't have the same amount of shut eye.

The link between memory recall and sleep has been examined very closely by many different researchers and it is thought that when you sleep, your brain effective resets itself. This means that if you want to remember something or even learn something new, you're going to have better results. Conversely, if you're tired and lacking in sleep, the neurons within the brain experience a build up of electricity, as a result of not being able to reset. This means that any new memories aren't saved as effectively, or at all.

This all means that focusing on sleep and placing it as a priory in your life is vital. Despite that, not everyone finds it easy to go to sleep quickly and stay that way for a solid 8 hours. There are a few things you can do to help however:

•   Have a regular bed time and waking up time and avoid those weekend lay ins

•   Have power naps if you feel tired during the day. Studies have shown that if you have a quick power nap after you've learnt something you want to remember, e.g. after a lecture, you're more likely to remember it

•   Avoid anything too simulating before bed, such as action movies, loud music, social media, or action games

•   Make sure that your room is comfortable for sleep, i.e. not too hot and not too cold and that you're able to get plenty of fresh air - sleeping with the window open just a little is often a good idea

•   Make sure your bed is comfortable and supportive and that your pillows don't cause you headaches and neck aches

•   You could try a weighted blanket if you struggle to get to sleep. Many people find these useful because they're relaxing, akin to a hug. When this happens, the brain releases a dose of dopamine, which actually helps you fall asleep much easier

•   Avoid eating too close to bedtime, and make sure you don't eat heavy meals in the three hours before you're planning to sleep

•   Try a warm, milky drink before bed; this helps some people

•   A warm bath is useful before bed too

•   Some people find lavender oil to be a relaxing alternative method for aiding sleep. A few drops on your pillow may help, but do check with your doctor if you have any contraindications to essential oil use

Move a Little More

You might wonder how getting more exercise does anything for your memory, but it's more than your body that's getting a workout.

When you exercise, your heart starts pumping extra oxygen around the body, via the bloodstream. This also makes it up towards the brain. The brain requires oxygen in order to work properly, so when you workout, you're feeding your brain quite effectively!

Many studies have shown that regular exercise, particularly aerobic exercise, can help to improve memory function. This is also because exercise causes cathepsin B, a naturally occurring protein, to be released. This protein feeds the hippocampus, which we know is so vital for memory function and growth.

Be Diet Savvy

Up to now, we know that you need to ensure you're getting enough sleep every night and move your body a little more, but you also need to watch your diet and make sure that you're getting enough of the right types of foods.

It makes a lot of sense when you think about it - improving your health by ensuring that you're getting the right vitamins and minerals benefits every part of your body, including your brain. However, there are certain foods which are thought to be more beneficial than others.

Saturated fat is linked to a decline in memory, just as trans-fats are. These are the types of fats that you'll find in excessive amounts of red meat, butter, and other processed foods. We know that cholesterol is bad for your body because it stick in your blood vessels and causes an increased risk of heart disease and stroke, but it can do the exact same thing to your brain.

The oxygen that your brain needs to function doesn't make it to the parts of the brain it needs to get to, and as a result, your memory is one of the first things to be affected. It's for this reason that you'll find studies linking plant-based diets with increased memory improvement, because of far less saturated and trans-fat content.

So, which foods should you be working into your diet for extra memory-boosting properties?

• Fatty varieties of fish - Sardines, trout and salmon are fantastic for boosting brain function because they're naturally high in omega 3 fatty acids. This is a type of fat which your brain needs to build new cells and many studies have shown that eating a regular amount of oily fish/fatty fish could help to reduce your chances of developing dementia or Alzheimer's in later life. If you're not a fish fan, you could consider taking a fish oil supplement instead.

• Coffee - But only in moderation! The caffeine content in coffee helps to keep you alert and focused, whilst the antioxidants which are naturally occurring also help to keep the brain strong and healthy.

• Berries - Adding some berries to your morning porridge is a great idea, especially if you opt for blueberries. These are high in antioxidants and contain anthocyanin, which is a natural anti-inflammatory. This helps to reduce the effects of stress on the brain, and may help to reduce the chances of degenerative conditions, such as dementia.

• Turmeric - This is a delicious spice that you'll find easily these days and it's extremely antioxidant and anti-inflammatory. Turmeric is also able to cross into the brain directly, so you're getting direct benefits as a result. Regularly enjoying turmeric may help reduce your chances of developing Alzheimer's in later lifeboat may also help to improve your mood and encourage the grow of new brain cells.

• Broccoli - This is another natural food which is packed with antioxidants, whilst also containing a huge dose of vitamin K. This vitamin helps to encourage the growth of new brain cells and also improves memory in general.

• Pumpkin seeds - Sprinkle some of these on your yogurt or your porridge for major memory benefits! Pumpkin seeds are antioxidant and they help to protect against damage from free radicals, whilst also containing a good dose of copper, iron, zinc and magnesium. These are all powerful minerals for brain and memory function.

• Dark chocolate - Before you get excited, this literally means just a square or two per day and no more! Despite that, dark chocolate contains a high cocoa content and that in itself is an antioxidant because of the flavonoid contained within it. This helps to slow down decline of memory and brain function over time and improves cognitive function generally.

•   Nuts - A handful of nuts can help to boost your heart health, therefore ensuring that oxygen reaches the brain, whilst also helping to slow down mental decline during the aging process. Many studies have linked regular nut consumption to memory improvement, especially walnuts, as they contain omega 3 fatty acids, just like fish. Many nuts also contain vitamin E and antioxidants.

•   Eggs - Eggs contain B12, B6, choline and folate, which are all ideal for helping to boost the health of your brain and memory. Whilst the entire egg is ideal, the yolk is best if you're looking to get your daily amount of choline. Believe it not, eggs also help to keep your mood upbeat and stable!

•   Green tea - This is a beverage which we're all aware of in terms of health and wellbeing but it's ideal for brain and memory function too. This is because green tea contains L-theanine which is an important animo acid with the ability to cross into the brain directly. Green tea is a great natural relaxant but it also contains antioxidants which help to avoid stress damage in the brain.

•   Water - If you don't drink enough water you can easily become dehydrated and when that happens, you cannot focus or concentrate. Drinking plenty of water is vital for overall health and wellbeing but many people fail to do so. The general consensus is that 8 glasses of water per day is enough, falling into the 8 x 8 rule (8 x 8oz glasses).

These are all foods and beverages which are easy to incorporate into your diet and none of them are particularly unusual or lacking in taste! Being more aware of the foods which may affect your memory function adversely and reducing them in your diet is key, as well as increasing your intake of the foods and beverages which can help boost the health of your brain and memory in general.

Points to Remember From This Chapter

We've covered a lot of health and lifestyle-related information in this chapter, but all of it is vital if you want to cover the basics.

You cannot work towards a quality memory if you don't have a strong and healthy foundation to work on. Giving your brain the vitamins and minerals it needs to function effectively will always help you to store memories effectively and recall them when you need to, whilst giving you the concentration and focus you need to be productive throughout your day.

The main points to remember from this chapter are:

• Your brain needs vitamins and minerals to function healthy, just as your physical body does
• Alcohol can impair your memory, however one glass of wine won't hurt
• Illegal drugs used recreationally are extremely damaging for memory and brain function, as well as for overall health. This needs to stop immediately if this is something you use
• Focusing on sleep quality is vital if you want to be alert and focused. 7 to 8 hours of quality sleep per night is your aim
• Moving your body more, i.e. getting more exercise, will help to boost the flow of blood and oxygen to the brain, delivering nutrients and boosting your memory function

- Foods which contains a high amount of saturated and trans-fats are unhealthy choices for your brain
- There are many healthy foods which help to boost your brain function, and increasing your daily intake will help to improve your memory function
- Ensuring you get enough water every day and avoiding dehydration is vital for overall health and wellbeing.

Chapter 5: SMART Memory Course Part 1 - Feed Your Brain

Now we're about to embark on the first week of our SMART Memory Course. The hard work starts here, but the results will be more than worth the effort!

This course is going to take five months in total, so you could say it's 'five months to a better memory', and by then you will have learnt all the tools to allow you to improve your memory and have a greater level of general cognitive function.

Of course, it's going to take time and it's going to require a lot of effort, but the results will start to show overtime. Don't expect miracles overnight, and know that with every new exercise you learn and every new memory-boosting endeavor your attempt, you're working towards a snowball effect of increased memory function.

By the end of the five months you'll be able to look back over your hard work with pride, provided you put the hours in!

SMART MEMORY COURSE
INTRODUCTION

The next five chapters will cover one month each, and every week you will have tasks to complete. Some of these tasks are exercises, some are lifestyle changes, and some are tasks you need to revisit from previous weeks. Remember, when it comes to rewiring the brain, repetition is key. So, when you see a week containing something you've worked on during a past week, don't skip it. It's vital that you complete every week as stated, and repeat tasks and information as instructed to do so.

In this first month, we're going to focus on the basics. This means feeding your brain the nutrients it needs to work in a strong and healthy manner. Whilst we're not going to introduce a new memory-boosting exercise per se, we are going to go over some of the simple exercises we talked about in our previous chapter.

So, this first month might seem exercise-light, but that's because it's focusing on the foundations you're going to build on. By taking the time to complete each week as stated, you'll notice increased brain capacity as the weeks go on. Despite that, it's vital to be honest with yourself and take a long, hard look at your lifestyle right now, identifying improvement points you can make for the weeks ahead. Remember, lifestyle changes are designed to be long-term and not quick fixes!

This course is designed to be quite thought-provoking. It's not particularly heavy on tasks, however the final month of the course might stretch you a little as we introduce one of the more complicated memory improvement strategies. What the course is designed to do is to get you thinking, get you learning and creating and to help you use your imagination a little more. As you go through each week of the course, you'll understand just how important and the ability to visualize is, to boosting and improving your memory performance.

If you need to make notes as you go along, do so. Grab a pen and paper and scribble away, however you're free to scroll back and forth and re-read any points that you perhaps don't grasp the first time, or maybe you need to recap on as we move through.

If you skim through the tasks first, you'll notice that we introduce new methods and then recap on them a few weeks later. This is deliberate. Remember, the brain needs repetition in order to learn and commit information to the long-term memory bank. From there it can be recalled whenever necessary. Simply learning something once and then expecting to remember it is like walking in the rain without an umbrella and expecting not to get wet!

So, when you're ready, make yourself comfortable and let's get started with the very first week of the SMART Memory Course!

WEEK 1

Welcome to the first week of the SMART Memory Course. We'll ease you in gently to begin with, but this week requires you to be open and honest about your lifestyle and what you're currently feeding your brain.

The tasks for this week are:

- Keep a food diary
- Increase your intake of memory-boosting foods and drinks
- Focus on increasing your water intake

In order for your brain to function in the healthiest possible way, you need to give it what it needs. In our previous chapter on lifestyle, we talked about the fact that your brain needs certain nutrients and vitamins in order to function correctly and without those, your general health and wellbeing is far lower. As a result, you're not going to be able to think as clearly and your general cognitive function, concentration, focus and memory function is going to be reduced as a result.

This first week of the SMART Memory Course is dedicated to brain care. Think of it as self care but directed towards your skull!

Task 1 - Keep a Food Diary For One Week

Over the course of this first week you're going to write down everything that you eat and drink during the course of each of the seven days. The reason for this is because there are certain foods which are good for your memory and brain function, and there are foods and drinks which are less favorable. Identifying how many of the less favorable items you're consuming allows you to reduce them and therefore start on a positive foundation.

Grab yourself a notebook and dedicate a page to each day. You need to write down what you have for breakfast, dinner and lunch, any snacks you have, and include beverages throughout the day - yes, even that sneaky can of cola you drink in the afternoon needs to be written down too! You should also write down how much water you're drinking, which will help you with another of this week's aims, which we'll cover shortly.

When you reach the end of the week, look at your diary and work out what you need to eradicate from your diet or reduce as much as possible.

The types of foods and drinks you need to try and avoid are:

• 	Sugary types of drinks - This doesn't mean you have to stop drinking cola and other carbonated beverages completely, but it means you need to try and cut them down as much as you can. By 'sugary drinks' we mean things like soda, energy drinks, fruit juice and sports drinks, as well as cola-type drinks. This will benefit your health because these types of drinks (even fruit juice) are laden with sugar and help to increase your risk of obesity, heart disease and type II diabetes. Of course, this increased sugar intake also means your brain function may be affected, and over time may add to your risk of developing dementia and Alzheimer's. Drinks which contain fructose are also linked with brain inflammation and memory reduction.

•   Refined carbohydrates - This is quite a wide-ranging category, but refined carbs basically means carbohydrates which include sugars within them, as well as grains which are processed to a greater degree. This means you need to reduce your intake of white flour and instead replace them with healthier, low GI carbs, such as vegetables, whole grains and fruits. Refined carbs often have a high GI level, which means they're broken down by the body quite quickly and your blood sugar spikes as a result. This increase insulin levels within the body, and these types of foods have also been linked with reduced brain function over time.

•   Trans-fats - It's easy to become confused with the different types of fats and not all fats are dangerous or bad. However, trans-fats are an unsaturated fat which has been shown to affect the health and function of the brain. When used in foods such as shortening, frosting, margarine, pre-packaged baked goods and snacks, trans-fats can become dangerous if you eat too much of them, with a higher risk of Alzheimer's and a less than effective memory function.

•   Processed foods - We know that processed foods are unhealthy because they increase the risk of obesity and associated problems, but they can also affect the brain and memory function as a result. We're talking about foods like ready meals, pre-packed sauces, sweets, chips, and noodles. In addition, processed foods can affect the production of the BDNF molecule which is vital for memory function within the hippocampus. When this is reduced, memory is affected. Instead of processed foods, stick with fresh produce and learn to cook your own meals rather than relying upon shop bought ready meals - they're far tastier!

• Aspartame - Aspartame is an artificial sweeter and it is often found in products which label themselves as 'sugar-free'. In this case, you're replacing dangerous sugar with dangerous sweetener! Aspartame is able to cross the blood-brain barrier and as a result may cause problems with the neurotransmitters within the brain and memory overall. Aspartame is also a stressor for brain chemicals, which could cause issues over time.

• Alcohol - We've already talked about alcohol and how it is detrimental for memory, so it makes sense to add it to this list and ask you to reduce your alcohol level overall. We're not suggesting you stop drinking completely, but remember that moderation is key if you want to be fit and healthy, whilst enjoying the odd tipple every now and again.

• Fish containing high levels of mercury - Not all fish is great for brain function. On our healthy list we mentioned oily and fatty fish, but fish which has a high mercury level needs to be eradicated from your diet as much as possible. There are certain types of fish which can hold a huge amount of mercury within their body and this is a neurological type of poison. The effects are not pleasant at all and in order to avoid this huge issue you need to be mercury savvy. Whilst most types of fish are perfectly fine to consume, stick to just 2 to 3 servings of fish per week, unless its swordfish or shark, in which case one serving is enough.

Other types of fish to be particularly focused on including tuna, orange roughy, tilefish and king mackerel. As long as you stick to the recommended amounts, you should be fine.

In your diary, identify how many of the above types of foods you eat and then over the coming weeks, work to reduce them out of your diet either drastically or completely.

Task 2 - Increase Your Intake of Memory-Boosting Foods And Drinks

Your second task of this first week is to start adding in some of the memory boosting foods and drinks we mentioned in our earlier lifestyle chapter. Too refresh your memory, those foods and drinks included:

- Fatty/oily types of fish, such as sardines, trout and salmon
- Coffee (in moderation)
- Berries, especially blueberries
- Turmeric
- Broccoli
- Pumpkin seeds
- Dark chocolate (in moderation)
- Nuts, especially walnuts
- Eggs, especially the yolk
- Green tea

You can start by having fish perhaps twice per week for dinner, add some berries to your morning porridge or yogurt during a snack, and drink green tea in replacement of regular tea mid-morning. Snack on nuts in the afternoon rather than reaching for a bag of sweets, and add a side of broccoli to your dinner a couple of times per week.

As you can see, it's not hard to incorporate these types of foods into your diet, and they're all super-delicious too!

So, from your food diary, you need to work towards limiting the negative foods and increasing the positive ones.

Task 3 - Focus on Increasing Your Water Intake

Week one's final task is around water intake.

We mentioned earlier that you need to focus on drinking 8 x 8oz glasses of water every day.

Buy a refillable water bottle and fill it up on a regular basis, keeping it on your desk or in your bag so you can sip throughout the day. Drink water instead of sugary drinks with your meals and challenge yourself to simply dry and drink more of Mother Nature's H2O in general.

Staying hydrated ensures that you're healthy but it also boosts memory function and general brain health overall. If you find that you don't like the bland taste of water, you can add in a drop of lemon juice, lime juice, or even the juice of an orange. Provided you're not using packaged fruit juices (remember, they contain extra sugars and fructose), you'll increase the taste and get plenty of benefit too.

WEEK 2

You've made it to week 2, well done! By now you should be feeling a little more energized and healthier than you did beforehand, thanks to a week of feeding your brain and rehydrating.

It goes without saying that whatever you started to do in your first week, you need to continue during the second week and onwards. That goes for any advice or exercise we give you throughout the book - when the week is over, don't just forget about it, keep using the tools and advice and allow them to become repetitive actions that cement themselves in your brain.

This week we're going to continue the healthy brain theme by focusing on sleep and relaxation.

Your tasks for this week are:

- Keep a sleep diary and identify any trouble spots
- Create a comfortable sleeping environment
- Use deep breathing techniques for relaxation

It's impossible to have a clear mind and good memory if you're tired, foggy, and exhausted. We've already touched upon the benefits of sleep in our lifestyle chapter, and from there you will know that you need to aim for 7 to 8 hours of uninterrupted sleep every evening.

Task 1 - Keep a Sleep Diary

It's important to know what your starting point is, so just like you did in the first week, you now need to keep a diary, albeit for something a little different. This diary is going to focus on sleep. That means you need to measure how much sleep you're getting, whether or not it was interrupted, how easy or hard you found it to fall asleep, and you could even write down any troubling dreams you had. It's also useful to write down the things you ate before bed and at what time.

Focusing on sleep isn't just about saying "oh I slept last night", it's also about looking at the quality and working out where you need to focus your attention. Some people don't realize that they're suffering from sleep quality problems until they start to record things and then look back at patterns. By doing this, you can identify if you need to perhaps start turning the TV off a little earlier before bed, cutting out foods you eat before bed, and if things look like they need a little extra help, you could even go and see your doctor and talk about possible insomnia treatments.

By being more sleep savvy, you're able to give your brain the rest it needs of an evening, therefore allowing you to increase your brain function without really trying. However, it's a good idea to wait until a full week has passed before looking for patterns in your sleeping situation, as we all have the odd bad night's sleep occasionally and that doesn't necessary mean there's a problem per se.

Task 2 - Create a Comfortable Sleeping Environment

Our second task means looking at your sleeping environment and working out whether you can make any changes to give you a better sleeping situation.

We talked about the best sleeping environment in our lifestyle chapter, but this task is about looking at what you have and making changes. So, if the room warm enough or too cold? Do you need to open the window, or do you need to change the central heating to make it a little cooler at night? Does the central heating come on a certain time I the morning, therefore waking you up because the temperature quickly increases?

In addition, do you need to change your pillows? Do you need a new duvet? What changes do you think you can make which will give you a better and more comfortable sleeping environment? This isn't about being cosy, it's about giving your body the comfort it needs to relax enough to fall into a deep enough sleep for your brain to have the relaxation and regeneration time it needs.

Task 3 - Use Deep Breathing Techniques For Relaxation

Stress is not good for anyone or anything, and that includes your memory. It could also be that stress is affecting your sleep quality, causing you to fall into a disrupted sleep, or making it hard to fall asleep in the first place.

In order to combat that, deep breathing exercises can help.

Before bed every day, try this relaxation exercise:

•   Sit or lay down somewhere comfortable and make sure you're not going to be disrupted
•   Close your eyes and turn your attention to your breath
•   Observe how your abdomen rises and falls with every breath
•   As thought come into your mind, don't pay them any attention and simply allow them to float back out
•   Breathe in through your nose for a count of five, in a slow and steady manner
•   Pause for a count of five
•   Exhale through your mouth for a count of five, in the same manner
•   Repeat until you feel calm

You could also add in a visualization technique here. You can imagine your breath as a color and watch it rise and fall as you focus on your breath.

This is all very relaxing and calming, helping you to battle stress and also allow your mind to chill out to the point where you're ready to fall asleep. Try it for a week and see how you feel; the chances are you'll start to feel less stressed and you'll also have a tool which will allow you to handle stressful situations as they come into your life.

Week 3

The third week of the SMART Memory Course is going to slowly move us towards the practical side. This week we're going to focus on the Mind Map technique we mentioned a little earlier in the book, introducing it into your routine and using it for the first time to remember something important to you. We're also going to continue our focus on health and wellbeing, giving you the best foundation on which to start your memory-boosting journey.

Your tasks for this week are:

- Consider the use of supplements
- Use the Mind Map technique to remember something important
- Be mindful of continuing the lifestyle changes you've made over the last few weeks

Task 1 - Think About Using Necessary Supplements

Now, this particular task isn't by any means something you have to do, but it's something you should think about and do some research into.

There are certain situations when taking supplements to boost brain and memory function is a good idea. For instance, we've already talked about the fact that omega 3 acids you get from oily or fatty fish is a serious brain booster, but not everyone likes the taste of fish. In that case, a supplement could be a good option to help you get those vitamins, without having to eat a food you really don't enjoy.

However, before you consider taking any supplement, you need to talk to your doctor, especially if you have any medical conditions or you're taking any medications. Most people are fine to take supplements, but it's always better to check, just in case the supplement you're planning on taking is contraindicated in your case. Once you get the green light, you can start to do your research.

To give you an idea of a few supplements you can look into, some of the best for brain and memory function are:

- Omega 3 fatty acids, via fish oil supplements or krill oil
- Resveratrol
- Caffeine
- Phosphatidylserine

- Acetyl-L-Carnitine
- Ginkgo Biloba
- Creatine
- Bacopa Monnieri
- Rhodiola Rosea
- S-Adenosyl Methionine

Of course, you need to look into each one of these carefully and assess their pros and cons for your specific situation before you make a choice. Some are better at memory improvement than others, some have more memory decline protection than others, and some are focused on alertness more than others. Reading about specific supplements and talking to your doctor about which one might be best for you will give you the best chance at using a supplement for the greater good.

However, all of this doesn't mean you have to go down the route of supplements if you don't want to. Some people are against supplements and if that's your situation, that's more than fine, this is totally option and may or may not give benefit to those who decide to try them out. For your first task this week however, we're just asking you to consider it and do some research.

Task 2 - Use The Mind Map Technique For The First Time

We've spent the last two weeks focusing on your health and giving your brain the best foundation it needs, and now we're going to test it out a little and make your memory do some work!

A little earlier in the book we talked about the mind map technique, and this is something you're now going to try for the first time in practice. It's best to do this early in the week, perhaps on Monday, and then try and test your recall of your mind map throughout the week. Remember, you might struggle at first, but the more you practice this technique (and any memory technique), the stronger your function and recall will become.

To give you a refresher, the mind map is a great technique for remembering a concept or a series of ideas. You'll need a piece of paper and a pen for this, and if you want to really boost your recall potential, you'll need some colored pens too.

Think of something you want to remember, perhaps your shopping list or a concept you're trying to learn for your studies or at work. Write a strong keyword in the middle of the page and draw a circle around it. Then, use small arrows shooting off the main central word with keywords that trigger other items you want to remember associated with it. For instance, if you're attempting to remember your shopping list, you could simply write 'dairy 3' and that would remind you to buy yogurt, milk and butter. Remember, this is your own mind map so the words and concepts you choose are going to be personal to you.

Make your map as colorful and inventive as you can. The more creative it is, the easier it will be to remember.

Once you've drawn it and you're happy, sit and look at it intently.

Try and commit the drawing to memory. Don't rush the memory, but instead focus on the different words and the creativity around them. Try and imagine it coming to life in front of you, the words moving and dancing. Remember, the more inventive you are, the more you're going to remember.

After a while, turn it over and close your eyes. Can you see it clearly in front of you? Zoom in on it in your mind's eye and try and remember the words. If you're struggling look at it again and repeat the committing to remember side. Test it out again.

Once you're sure that you can remember it, fold the mind map up and put it somewhere you can find it. This could be your bag, your pocket, your wallet, wherever. The idea isn't that you never need to look at the piece of paper, it's that you can remember it as much as possible without referring to it, but that if you do look at the paper, the keywords trigger connections in your mind and you know what they mean without having to wrack your brain.

Test your first run of the mind map technique out as you move through the week.

Task 3 - Be Mindful of Your Lifestyle Changes

Over the last two weeks you've made some great and very positive changes to your diet and your sleeping habits, and in our following week we're going to focus on adding some exercise to that too. However, your third task for this week is to be mindful of the changes you've made and commit to continuing them.

Give yourself a pat on the back and congratulate yourself, but don't let the novelty factor kick in and then wear off. These are changes you need to make for the rest of your life, in order for them to be useful and long-lasting.

It might be useful to review your changes in a few weeks to see if they're making much of a difference to how you feel and how easily you are able to focus and recall details, using the new strategies we're going to introduce as we move throughout the course. You'll notice that some of our future tasks do include recapping on changes you've made, but this is something you should also be mindful of and doing continually, especially if you notice any adverse changes to your health, or how you feel in general. Everything you change should be for your benefit, not only for your health, but also for your happiness and your general wellbeing too.

So, your final task for this third week of the SMART Memory Course is to look back over your progress so far and be mindful of your changes, patting yourself on the back, and vowing to continue.

Week 4

You're almost at the end of the first month!

This first month has focused on health and wellbeing, whilst also adding in the odd exercise. This fourth week is going to continue that theme, preparing you for the coming weeks. In the next four months to come, we're going to introduce a specific new technique every month. We'll then spend the weeks within each month practicing it and honing your skills, whilst also using other methods from the previous weeks in repetition to strengthen those connections in your memory.

This week however, we're going to look at the role of exercise, whilst trying another technique for the first time.

Your tasks for this week are:

- Move your body a little more
- Find an exercise you enjoy
- Use the Sound Alike Method for the first time

Task 1 - Move Your Body

In our lifestyle chapter we talked about the role of exercise in general health and wellbeing but how getting your heart pumping also brings fresh oxygen and nutrients to the brain. This week we're going to dedicate ourselves to moving a little more and that's your first task to focus on.

Do you drive to work? If so, how about walking every other day if possible? If it's too far, how about parking the car a few blocks away and walking the last few minutes? These small changes will make a big difference to your health in general, but will also allow you to feel more focused when you arrive at work that morning.

Do you take the elevator rather than the stairs on a regular basis? Unless you work on the very top floor of a skyscraper building, it's time to ditch the elevator and walk up and down the stairs instead. You don't have to run, you simply need to take your time and move your body a little more. Again, this might seem like a small change, but the more you do it, the greater the rewards.

Another suggestion is to go for a walk on your lunch break, rather than sitting in the cafeteria and reading a gossip magazine or checking your social media feeds. It's far more productive to head outside and get some fresh air, whilst moving your body on a walk around the block. Again, you'll feel more focused when you go back to work that afternoon and you'll have clocked up some extra steps for the day.

There are many ways you can move your body a little bit more, and it doesn't necessarily means you have to hit the gym to do it. Make small changes to your day and you'll notice the results.

On the first day of this week, write down three aims for the week to help you get moving a little more than before. This could be walking to work, going for a lunch time walk, going swimming after work a couple of times during the week, or avoiding the elevator. Write down your aims and make sure you tick them off your list.

Task 2 - Find an Exercise You Can Enjoy Over The Long Term

Moving on from the small changes to your day, this week is also going to be the week you choose a new exercise and dedicate time to it every week following. This doesn't have to be enrolling in the gym, however if you want to do that, that's more than fine too.

A few suggestions include:

- Swimming
- Walking
- Jogging
- Yoga
- A team sport you enjoy
- An exercise class, such as Zumba

Just choose one and dedicate one or two evenings of your week to an hour or so enjoying it. Make sure that it is something you enjoy and not simply something you're doing for the sake of it. In order to make this a regular part of your routine, it has to be enjoyable!

In conjunction with the general idea of moving your body more, you'll find that your new exercise dedication helps your overall health, gives you more energy, and also boosts your brain function at the same time.

So, what do you enjoy now? Is there a way you can do more of that, or make time for it? If you're not sure what exercise you would like to choose, how about having a chat with a close friend and seeing if you can tag along with something they do, perhaps a team sport, a jogging session after work, or just a walk with the dogs and a good chat as you do so? Moving your body more doesn't have to be full-on cardio, it simply needs to mean that you get your heart rate up, your breathing up a little, and perhaps even sweat a little!

Task 3 - Use the Sound Alike Method For The First Time

Last week we started using the mind map method and that is something you need to continuing doing over the coming weeks. This week we're going to introduce the Sound Alike method for the first time, giving you another technique to use when you need to remember something small, such as a name.

As before, we did run through the basics of this method in our earlier chapter but let's recap again.

If you want to remember a name, a place or a small detail, picture it in your mind clearly. Now, come up with something which rhymes with that name, or sounds very much like it. For instance, if you wanted to remember the name Carol, you could picture the actor Colin Farrell. That might sounds crazy, but Farrell sounds a lot like Carol, and the more obscure the link, the more you're likely to remember it!

So, you could then add Colin Farrell to your picture of Carol;

perhaps they could be holding hands. Visualize it in your mind and repeat 'Carol, Colin Farrell' in your mind, or aloud if you can. Focus and really try and commit that detail to your memory.

Test it out over the day and keep saying Colin Farrell, to see what pops up. After a few times, it's not likely to be an image of Mr Farrell himself that comes to your mind, but Carol herself!

Again, test it out over the week and assess your progress as the week ends. You can also try other names and information too, using different visualization and words to create new connections you can try and recall the following week.

Remember, just because Sound Alike might not be on the plan for next week (you'll see whether or not it is in our next chapter), that doesn't mean you shouldn't still practice it. Keep using all the techniques repeatedly when we introduce them, to increase your chances of these methods working for you over time.

And with that, you've come to the end of the first month. Pat yourself on the back and congratulate yourself for having the dedication to a month of improving your memory. You've done well and hopefully you'll have noticed some small changes in how you feel and how able you are to recall memories. However, that doesn't mean you're finished or it's time to give in! You have another four months in front of you, giving you a full five months towards a better brain.

Points to Remember From This Chapter

This has been your first month of practical lessons. The main points to take from this chapter are:

•   Feeding your brain what it needs is vital if you want to improve your memory

•   The basics are just as important as the depth techniques we're going to cover in the coming months

•   Focusing on cutting out the negative brain foods and increasing the positive ones is the first step

•   Focus on sleep and exercise to complete your lifestyle overhaul

•   You may consider adding in supplements if you want to, but this is not a necessity if you're against it, or if you have any medical contraindications - you need to discuss this with your doctor before you begin, and before you identify a specific supplement you think you might like to take

•   All the exercises and tasks we give you need to be repeated beyond the introduction week. For instance, you need to continue practicing the mind map method beyond the week we gave it to you as a task - repetition is key if you want to build new connections and develop your memory.

Chapter 6: SMART Memory Course Part 2 - The Acronym Method

You're now on to your second month of the SMART Memory Course and by now you should be noticing at least some effects from the hard work you've put in so far.

Up until this point we have focused on health and wellbeing, giving you a firm foundation on which to start your memory improvement endeavors. In this, your second method of memory training, we're going to introduce a brand new strategy, called the Acronym Method. This method has two different variants, the Acronym Mnemonic Technique and the Sentence Method. Both of these methods are quite similar but they're useful for different types of information.

Remember, you should continue to use and practice the tasks you were given in the first month of training. We should also point out that we're basing this program on four weeks in every month, but some months do have five weeks. In that case, you can use the extra week in a particular method to recap on what you've learnt that month and do a little extra practice!

So, let's gets started with month two, starting back at week number one. You will notice that this month you have less tasks to complete in one week, but these are more intensive tasks that require more practice in order to help them work for you. Our last month was about lifestyle changes so you could easily more in the space of a week, however this month you're going to need to learn new techniques and practice them across the space of the seven days in front of you.

Week 1

A very useful method to help you remember slightly larger pieces of information is the Acronym Mnemonic Method. This falls under the umbrella of the general Acronym Method, but this is one half of the puzzle; we'll learn the Sentence Method next week.

This week we're going to learn how using mnemonics and acronyms can help you recall information quickly. This can be a series of names, a piece of information or facts.

Your tasks for this week are:

- Introduce and start using the Acronym Mnemonic Method
- Remember a phone number with a jingle

Task 1 - Introduce and start using the Acronym Mnemonic Method

We use acronyms almost every day, especially in technology and text speak. For example, LOL (laugh out loud) or BRB (be right back) are acronyms which are used to shorten speech but they can also be used to help you remember things too.

An acronym is made up of the first letters of the word you want to remember. For instant, SMART is an acronym for setting goals, and it covers the first letters of the words that are associated with each step. In this case:

Specific
Measurable
Attainable
Relevant
Timely

When setting goals for yourself, you would ensure that you hit every single one of those requirements and you would use the acronym SMART to remember what you need to do.

Can you think of an acronym for something you need to remember? That is your first task for this week. It can be anything, but try and make an acronym out of the first letters of the words you need to remember.

For instance, if you wanted to remember your grocery list, you might think of something like this:

Milk
Oranges
Bread
Yoghurt

In that case, your acronym would be MOBY, and you would use it when you get to the store to remember to buy milk, oranges, bread, and yoghurt.

It's a good idea to arrange the words you want to remember into a series of letters that actually form a sensical word. Of course, you can opt for a word that doesn't exist if you want, but it's often easier to remember the associated words when the acronym actually means something in general.

So, your first task for this week is to come up with an acronym for something you need to remember and practice using it throughout the week. Notice if you seem to remember certain acronyms better than others, e.g. made up words versus genuine words, and try and tweak your efforts to make sure that you improve your performance as the week goes on. This will help you to make easier to remember acronyms in the future, when you need to remember lists or large amounts of information.

The point of the acronym method is that it helps to form connections in the brain. You'll remember that we talked about this when mind mapping, and the keywords you write down then trigger a memory of what that word is about. For instance, you might write down the word 'packing' and it will remind you that you need to buy a new suitcase for your upcoming vacation, etc. These types of exercises strengthen the connections between information in your brain and therefore improve your memory over time.

Task 2 - Remember a Phone Number With a Jingle

Your second task this week goes back to the quick memory improvement methods we talked about in an earlier chapter - using jingles to remember information.

Your senses are very strongly linked to your memory and music in particular can be very powerful when it comes to remembering pieces of information. As we explored earlier, it is for this reason that advertisers come up with catchy jingles - they want that jingle to stick in your mind and make you remember the product they're trying to sell. It's almost subliminal!

This week you're going to try and remember a telephone number using a jingle.

It can be any type of tune, upbeat and fun, slow and chilled out, whatever you can remember best. However, the more fun you make it, the catchier you make it, the more likely it is to stick in your head.

Think about the famous Baby Shark song, for example. It didn't really make you remember anything in particular because that wasn't the aim, but it stuck in your mind because the tune was repetitive and really quite annoying! That is what you're aiming for - something which embeds itself in your mind, helping you to recall the numbers quickly.

Create your jingle on the first day of the week and then sing it to yourself repeatedly throughout the week. See how easily you recall the telephone number at the end of the week. The more you practice, the more you push this number into your brain, the easier it will be to recall via the medium of a jingle.

Of course, it's likely to get stuck in your head and become an annoyance, but you have to realize that's the main point of a jingle! Jingles aren't designed to be melodic and fun, they're designed to be so annoyingly catchy that they stick in your head and no matter what you do, you can't seem to shake it. Your aim is to come up with a jingle that is so annoying, it rivals Baby Shark, and helps you remember whatever it is you're trying to commit to your memory bank. Let your imagination run free!

Week 2

How did you feel using the Acronym Mnemonic Method last week? Did you find it useful? This week we're going to move on from that particular method and introduce its sibling, the Sentence Method.

This method is very similar to the Acronym Mnemonic Method, but instead of just using the first letters of the words to create a new word, you're going to create a sentence. You've probably used this in the past, especially when you were at school. For instance, did you learn the colors of the rainbow using the sentence "Richard of York Gave Battle in Vain"?

This sentence reminds you that the colors of the rainbow, in order, are red, orange, yellow, green, blue, indigo and violet.

It's useful!

This week we're going to start using the Sentence Method, but you should continue looking for mnemonics and acronyms, as you did last week. By using them side by side, you'll keep your brain fresh and healthy, keep those new connections being developed, and you'll find ways which suit you best. Much of this process comes down to trial and error at the start, and the more you try and find the different methods that suit you best, the better you'll be able to remember things.

Your tasks for this week are:

- Introduce and start using the Sentence Method
- Revisit your diet and see if you can add in any extra healthy brain foods

Task 1 - Introduce And Start Using The Sentence Method

We're going to give the Sentence Method a try now.

As you've just learned, the Sentence Method creates fun and quirky sentences out of information you need to remember. As with the Acronym Mnemonic Method, this can be very useful when you'e trying to remember large amounts of information in one quick and easy attempt. Another good example of a sentence used to memorize information is My Dear Aunt Sally. This helps you to remember the mathematical order, e.g. multiply and divide, and then add and subtract.

Your first task for this week is to come up with a sentence that helps you remember a larger amount of information. This can be anything. We used the example of your shopping list when coming up with the MOBY acronym last week, so mix things up a little this week and avoid trying to remember your shopping list in this way. How about remembering the order you need to complete some tasks?

A good example of that could be:

"I pat warm feet"

Random, yes, but it helps you remember the following information:

Ironing, pay electric bill, do the washing, and fill out your tax return.

Come up with something original to you and your day or your week, but give it a go. Then, at the end of the week try and work out whether you like the Acronym Mnemonic Method best or the Sentence Method. Which comes easier to you? Which did you find easier to recall? Do you think that's down the information you're trying to remember or the fact that one method suits you best personally?

Exploring these questions will help you to find your ideal memory recall method for future use. Of course, it could also be that you find both equally as useful, which is quite the bonus!

Task 2 - Revisit And Review Your Diet

Your second task for the week is to go back over your diet from last month and see if you can make any changes, add in any new memory-boosting foods, and basically assess your progress.

It's a good idea to look back over changes you've made and review them, as it helps you to address any problems and look for further ways to improve.

So, how many of the foods we mentioned in last month's diet section have you managed to add in to your diet? Can you try and add in some more? Are you finding that you're drinking enough water, or do you need help to try and remember?

At this point, be honest about your dietary effects and see what changes you can make. You've been working on this for a few weeks now, so this is the ideal time to do a little honest reviewing and work out what could be done better, or pat yourself on the back for a job well done.

You will remember that last month we mentioned we would continually revisit lifestyle changes and see how you're doing. This is the first check in we're doing, but that doesn't mean you should forget about it afterwards. Keep monitoring your diet, see how you feel, watch your energy levels, and see if you can keep adding in new foods and new ingredients into your meals. You never know, perhaps you think you don't like a specific food, but once you try it in a different way, perhaps as part of a recipe, you'll love it! It doesn't matter how you eat it, as long as you get it into your diet on a recurring basis!

WEEK 3

You're almost at the end of your second month and that means you should certainly be seeing some positive effects by now. Take a moment to think back over your progress and pat yourself on the back. No improvement journey should be taken without a quick 'well done' for everything you've achieved!

This week we're going to further reinforce the Acronym Mnemonic Method by helping you to remember a few names in order and we're also going to look back over your exercise efforts and see what changes could be made, if any are needed at all.

Your tasks for this week are:

•	Remember the names of your work colleagues using the Acronym Mnemonic Method

•	Introduce a new exercise regime

Task 1 - Remember a List of Names Using The Acronym Mnemonic Method

The first week of this month we talked about the Acronym Mnemonic Method and we tried to remember your shopping list. That was your first attempt at using this memory memory, so it's a good idea to revisit it and use it to remember another piece of information. That's what your first task for this week involves.

We're going to assume that at work, you have several colleagues.

Whilst you probably know their names, you might find it hard to quickly put a name to a face when put on the spot. This is a particularly problem for people who work in large, open plan offices. To avoid embarrassing yourself and not being able to remember Doris from Purchasing's name, use an acronym to put those names to faces, by picturing the office in your mind.

We're using the work example for this exercise, but you can tweak it to a situation that suits your specific situation if you don't actually work in a large office. It's an example and you can see the general gist we're aiming for.

Try this:

Close your eyes and visualize your office. Remember the order of the desks in a clockwise position
Once you've got the image clear in your mind, recall who sits at each desk
Scribble down the first letters of their names - that will be your acronym

So, it might be:

Dave
Annabelle
Caroline
Eric
Linda

Your acronym would be DACEL

As you can see, it makes no sense as an actual word but it doesn't have to. That's not the point. The point is that the acronym stands in place of a regular word and give you the clockwise faces of people who sit inside your office - Dave, Annabelle, Caroline, Eric, and Linda. You're using visualization to add an image to that acronym, therefore strengthening it and allowing you to remember more information with just one method.

Give it go!

Let your imagination run free and come up with random words. As long as they stick in your mind there doesn't have to be any sense in them. Of course, it's probably easier to come up with a word that is actually in the dictionary, but you could also argue that obscure words are easier to remember because they have that 'weird' factor.

Everyone is different, so see which route works for you. Do you prefer to come up with your own combinations, perhaps words that aren't even in the dictionary, or do you prefer to use actual words that mean something to you? Work with both for a while and see which you recall easier.

Task 2 - Review Your Exercise Regime

Your second task for this week, whilst you're also trying to remember names and images is to look back over your exercise efforts and do a little review.

Last week we reviewed your diet, and this week we're going to do the same thing with your exercise. Are you getting enough exercise? Have you noticed yourself feeling more energized or fitter in general? Are you enjoying the exercise you chose for yourself? This week, why not introduce a new one, or take a break from the old exercise and give something new a go?

Refreshing your exercise regime means that you're no going to become bored of it and let it slip. Keep refreshing things and you'll find it easier to stick to them. In addition, see if you can entice a friend or family member to join you, especially if you're finding it hard to summon up the motivation on a regular basis. The social elements makes exercise more fun and actually takes your mind off the fact that you're giving yourself a work out!

WEEK 4

The final week of the second month is here! Another pat on the back is due. It's important that you keep congratulating yourself whenever you reach these milestones - you're working hard and praise is due!

This week we're going to further reinforce two specific strategies - the Sound Alike Method from earlier in the first month and we're going to add a little music to the Sentence Method to make it easier to remember longer pieces of information.

Remember, everything we've learned so far needs to be practiced throughout the following weeks. It is for this reason that we're giving you less new tasks to focus on every week, because the previous work needs to be practiced too!

Your tasks for this week are:

- Go back over the Sound Alike method
- Use The Sentence Method to create a song

Task 1 - Revisit the Sound Alike Method

Last month we talked about using the Sound Alike Method and adding in a little visualization to help you recall names, information, etc. Your first task of this week is to use that method again.

You cannot quickly learn a new method without constantly going back over it and whilst we've told you to keep practicing what you've learned, focusing on a specific technique in more detail means having it as a specific weekly task.

So, let's quickly summarize the Sound Alike Method here.

- The Sound Alike Method helps you remember information by coming up with a word which sounds a lot like the thing you want to remember
- You then add an image to that word, to further reinforce

the information you're trying to remember

Do you remember how to use the Sound Alike Method now? If not, go back over and read again in our chapter on daily memory-boosting methods. If you're pretty sure you can remember, make it your first task this week to practice this method a little more and try and remember a few more specific names, dates, addresses, etc.

Remember, this method is ideal for small pieces of information, so don't try and complicate it by trying to remember longer pieces of information or data.

Task 2 - Use the Sentence Method to Create a Song

Do you remember how we used a jingle to remember information a little earlier on? Is the jingle you invented still in your mind? It's likely to be, such is the power of music! Your second task for this week is to take the Sentence Method we've learned about this month and add a little music to it, creating a song alongside the information you're trying to remember. This will further strengthen the information you need to recall.

It's pretty easy to do this, but it really adds extra impetus on what you're trying to remember.

Let's take the 'Richard of York Gave Battle in Vain' sentence that is used to remember the order of the colors of the rainbow.

Now, you could simply say the words and still remember the information, but if you sing it, if you add a little internalized music to the words, it becomes more fun, a little quirky, and those are the easier to remember pieces of information we keep within our brains.

Go on, sing it! Make up a tune, add in a few funny sound effects, and repeat it in your mind until it sticks. Then, see how much easier you recall the information simply because you added in a musical push.

Points to Remember From This Chapter

This chapter has introduced two other memory methods - the Acronym Mnemonic Method and the Sentence Method. We've also revisited some of the other methods and helped to further enhance your understanding and practice. On top of that, we've looked back over your diet and your exercise regime to see if any changes can be made, or whether you've finally found the perfect blend for you.

The main points to take from this chapter are:

•   The Acronym Mnemonic Method and the Sentence Method are similar methods, and can be used to help remember larger amounts of information
•   The Acronym Mnemonic Method uses the first letter of the information to create a regular word, or a made up one
•   The Sentence Method uses the first letters of words you

want to remember, but takes it a step further by creating an easy to remember sentence

• Both of these methods help to trigger memory recall and strengthen connections in the brain.

Chapter 7: SMART Memory Course Part 3 - The Link System

Do you use your imagination very much in your day to day life? Or, more likely, do you stick to facts and logical thinking, pushing imaginary thoughts away?

Children use their imaginations all the time and they come up with weird and wonderful stories on the spot. As we grow a little older, we tend to put our imagination to one side, focusing on facts, logic and the things which make sense to us.

However, your imagination can be a very powerful tool, especially when it comes to triggering naturally creativity and also in terms of boosting your memory power. It's also fun to sit and let your mind naturally wander occasionally. Who knows what innovative ideas you might come up with if you simply dare to let your imagination wander and perhaps dream the impossible?

You're now onto your third month of the SMART Memory Course

and that means we're about to introduce another memory recall system. This month's focus is the Link System.

The Link System has two main methods within it - The Chain Link System and the Story Method. These are the methods we're going to introduce and use this month, but both require the use of your imagination in a very healthy dose. Don't worry if you've not tapped into the power of your imagination for a while, as we're going to address that head on too.

Both of these new methods use your imagination to create stories and links between different pieces of information. The more imaginative, weird and wonderful, the easier the information will be to remember. Do you remember when we introduced the Sound Alike Method and we said that the stranger the visualized image you can attach to a word, the easier you will remember it? The same advice works with the Link System.

You're basically creating links between pieces of information which allow you to remember them in sequence, therefore helping you to recall larger pieces of information or even memories. Over time, you'll find these stick in your memory bank without much effort, and you can continue to come up with new links to remember new items you want to add on top.

Our brains actually use the Link System when recalling memories from our past. Have you ever started thinking about one memory and then suddenly you recall a specie piece of information that makes you remember another memory attached slightly to it? That is how the Link System works too and by tapping into this, you can remember large pieces of information quite easily, provided you get back in touch with your childhood imagination!

WEEK 1

You're just over halfway through the course now, and you should certainly be using the techniques we've covered so far on a daily basis. Remember, you need to keep practicing these, but we're now going to introduce the Story Method, one half of the Link System.

If you're someone who is quite creative and enjoys being lost in a world of their own, this particular system will be very fitting for you and you'll probably find that it helps you to remember quite a lot of information, without very much effort. If you're not someone who uses their imagination very often, this system will help you unlock the power of your mind and therefore reintroduce you to the idea of creative thinking. You never know where your imagination might take you!

Your tasks for this week are:

- Introduce and start using the Story Method
- Practice visualization

Task 1 - Introduce And Start Using The Story Method

The Story Method is part of the Link Method. The clue is in the title as to what this method entails, as you will be creating a story which links information you want to remember together. The flow of the tale you weave helps to strengthen connections in your memory, pulling the pieces of information together and helping them to make sense to you.

The Story Method is a very personal memory boosting exercise, because it's not going to make sense to anyone else. Last month we talked about acronyms and sentences to remember pieces of information and these can be used by anyone to remember the same information, e.g. SMART for goals or 'Richard of York Gave Battle in Vain'. We all know what those words and acronyms are helping you to remember, but the Story Method allows you to create your own personal story, puling pieces of information together in a seamless tale.

Let's give you an example, to highlight how this method works.

Perhaps you're trying to remember the big capital cities in Europe. You could create an acronym or a sentence, and you could add a jingle to them to help you remember, but the Story Method can also be used, and is a far more effective way to keep the information in order and to attach vivid images to each one.

For instance, you could tell yourself a story where you wake up in London, enjoying everything the English capital has to offer, but after a few days you decide to jump on the Eurostar over to

Paris, visiting the Eiffel Tower and eating fresh pastries. You meet a Spanish waiter living in Paris who tells you all about Madrid, his home town in Spain, but he enjoys spending time in Berlin too, over in Germany.

The story goes on and on, but it includes all the capital cities you're trying to remember, the names of the countries they belong to, and small pieces of detail which will help to create a picture, therefore strengthening the tale you're telling. As a result, you're far more likely to remember this little jaunt across Europe.

It doesn't have to be cities or geography, it can be absolutely anything, but the Story Method is best used for several pieces of information which have a link that you want to highlight, or which don't have a link and you need to be imaginative enough to create one.

This week your task is to make up your own story, trying to remember several pieces of information you want to link together. Let your imagination run riot and create your own tale. If you want to write it down, you can do so, but it's equally as useful to just store it in your memory and try and recall it over the days to come. By the end of the week, see if you can remember the story in full and the information that it pertains to.

Task 2 - Practice Visualization

The Link System requires a certain amount of both imagination and visualization. For someone with a creative mind, this isn't difficult, but it might be something you need to practice a little first.

We've tried a little visualization when we covered the Sound Alike Method, but your second task for this week is to spend some time strengthening your visualization skills. This will allow you to use the Link System in particular far more effectively. This is system which requires connections to be built upon stories and images, and these aren't things you will have seen or experienced in real life. If you can learn how to visualize and trust what you're seeing, you'll find the Link System comes to you far more easily.

So, how can you practice visualization.

- Sit down and make yourself comfortable
- Make sure you're not distracted, e.g. you're waiting for a phone call, you're hungry, someone is about to come home, etc
- Close your eyes and concentrate on your breathing for a few minutes, to allow your mind to calm
- Now, let your mind wander and see where it takes you
- When you think of something, let it wander a little more and try and create images connected to that thought
- Imagine the finer details, such as how things sound, what they look like, what they feel like, how they smell etc. The more detail you can create, the stronger your visualization skills will become
- When you're ready to leave your visualization, slowly bring yourself back to the room and sit still for a few seconds before moving.

Improving your visualization skills will help you in techniques which require you to use images, such as the Story Method and the Chain Link Method we're going to go to talk about shortly. Set some time aside every few days to practice your visualization skills. You'll probably find that it comes becomes one of the most interesting and looked forward to parts of your day, as it allows you to relax, escape from day to day life, and use your imagination to live in a new and exciting world.

WEEK 2

The Story Method is probably one of the most enjoyable ones you've focused on so far. You might find that you enjoy this method so much that you want to continue on with it, but give the next one a chance too. Remember, this entire process is about giving you a range of different techniques you can go to whenever you want to remember different types of information.

With that in mind, this week we're going to introduce the Chain Link Method.

The Chain Link Method is still part of the Link Method but differs from the Story Method a little.

Your tasks for this week are:

- Introduce and start using the Chain Link Method
- Spend some time exploring your imagination

Task 1 - Introduce And Start Using The Chain Link Method

The Chain Link Method requires you to seriously get to grips with your imagination, but it's a fun method to use and you'll also benefit if you've continued to practice your visualization skills, set out as your second task last week.

The Chain Link Method is sometimes called the Chaining Method, but it's one and the same. This works well for helping to remember a random list of information, such as a shopping list, as one example.

You will have a random list of words, such as pizza, tomatoes, eggs, tissues, slippers, etc. As you can see, they're not related very closely and the list is extremely random. It's hard to remember a list like this by using other methods and even the acronym method would be difficult here, because you wouldn't think to link together slippers and tomatoes without something else to help you out!

The Chain Link Method however creates a chain, as the name suggests. It's hard to really explain it, and it's best to demonstrate with an example.

Let's take the shopping list we just mentioned. Your chain would therefore look like this:

- Pizza and tomatoes
- Tomatoes and eggs
- Eggs and tissues
- Tissues and slippers

As you can see, the last word is repeated before adding on another, exactly as you would do if you were creating a chain.

The words alone still don't mean very much, and now you need to tap into your imagination and create a visualized back story, to help strengthen the chain and therefore allow you to remember the words when you're out shopping.

It might go a little like this:

You head to a pizza store and you decide to go for the tomato pizza because it's your favorite, you're enjoying it but suddenly someone walks in and asks for boiled eggs! Boiled eggs in a pizza store? How strange! The main asking for eggs has a box of tissues in his hand and when you look down you see he is wearing slippers in the shape of two eggs.

It's weird, it's wonderful, and the more you repeat it in your mind, the more you remember the finer details. Then, when you head to the supermarket to do your shopping, you'll run through the story in your mind and the chain you've connected between the items will allow you to remember everything on your list.

It's very similar to the Story Method, but you're adding items in a chain, which is what sets it apart slightly.

Your task this week is to use the Chain Link Method in a situation that crops up. It might be best to use it with your shopping list first, as it's the most common sense place to use it. Give it a go and see whether you prefer this method or you like the Story Method best. You might find you quite like both and in that case, you can interchange whenever suits you.

Task 2 - Explore Your Imagination

As we grow older, we often find it harder to use our imagination. If you want to boost your memory however, you need to recapture that imagination and use it for your greater good!

Your second task for this week is to use your imagination more and more. This involves daydreaming, allowing your mind to wander and letting your imagination start with one small point and then build it up and up until you have a weird and wonderful image in your mind.

A good way to start using your imagination is before you go to sleep. When you're rested and ready to nod off for the evening, lay there and simply allow your thoughts to wander. Rather than focusing on what you need to do the next day or the things you didn't do during that day, fix on something which is small and seemingly insignificant. For instance, it could be that you encountered a small dog on the way to work who was yapping away at your heels.

Pick that image up and allow yourself to examine it a little more. What did the dog look like? Did they have any distinguishing features? Take yourself back to the moment but then allow your mind to embellish the details. Perhaps if the dog was black and white, make them green and yellow. Turn their head ten times bigger than their body, a little like the dog from the movie The Mask. Let them run around and gallop like a horse. Let your mind simply turn that small dog into a huge imaginary creature and go with it. Don't censor or tell yourself that it's ridiculous - just see where it takes you.

This is something you'll need to do on a regular basis, because the more you do it, the easier it becomes. The point of focusing on your imagination is that it will help you create visual markers in your memory far easier. For instance, if you're using the Sound Alike method and you're creating an image to go along with a name you're trying to remember, if you use your imagination a little and learn how to harness its power, you'll come up with equally as powerful images to trigger your memory.

WEEK 3

This week we're going to recap on a few useful points we introduced in our first few weeks of the SMART Memory Course. This means using the mind mapping theory once more and then looking back over your sleep record and seeing how you're doing. As we did with exercise and diet, your lifestyle is something you should continually monitor and make useful changes to, if you want to live the healthiest life possible.

Your tasks for this week are:

- Revisit Mind Maps
- Look back over your sleep routine

Task 1 - Revisit Mind Maps

In month one we talked about using mind maps to help you remember large amounts of information, by creating new connections in your memory. It's no good just doing this once and then expecting it to stick and whilst you know that you need to continue practicing every exercise we give you, this week's dedicated first task is to go back over mind maps and use them again.

You already know how to use mind maps, i.e. creating a colorful and visually stimulating map that sticks in your mind, with keywords to remind you of larger amounts of information, and you know to write this down and design it on paper, looking at it whenever you want to remember more about what the mind map is for.

So, come up with another model to use a mind map for. See if you have better results the second time around compared to the first. Did you use any other memory triggering points? Did you design it in a different way? Did you use more colors or did you use the same types of colors?

Compare the first time versus the second time and see if your approach brings you better results.

Task 2 - Are You Getting Enough Sleep?

Right at the very start, we encouraged you to make sure you're getting enough sleep. Did you keep a sleep diary? If so, look over it and see if you can find any new patterns, now you've been keeping it for a little longer.

How do you feel now? Do you feel more energized having got more sleep on a nightly basis? Do you feel that you have a greater memory and general concentration capacity as a result of being more rested? Are there any other changes you think you could make?

It's possible that you're still struggling with the odd night of sleeping difficult, and that's okay as long as you recognise it and try and fix the issue. Perhaps you could change your pillows or look towards a weighted blanket as an addition, part of this week's task. Or, maybe you could try a warm bath before bed and see if that makes any further improvement to your sleeping situation.

This week, spend some time looking back over the start of the first week and how well you were sleeping, compared to now. If you think there is still room for improvement (there normally is), then you can look towards making those changes now and then reviewing it again in a few weeks.

Week 4

You've almost completed another month! You're now three months into the SMART Memory Course and you should be seeing some results, although these will vary from person to person. In this, the final week of month three, you're going to look back over the two main strategies we introduced this month, as part of the Link System.

Your tasks for this week are:

• Use the Story Method to remember birthdays across the year

• Recall the Chain Link Method example you came up with from week 2

Task 1 - Use The Story Method to Remember

a Year's Worth of Birthdays

Think back to the first week of this month, when we introduced the Story Method. If you need to recap on that for a few minutes, simply head back and read through it again.

To summarize however, the Story Method is a way of creating a fun story to link together pieces of information. This week, we're going to use that remember important birthdays throughout the year.

This is something everyone forgets! We usually end up having reminders on our phone calendars to give us a head's up a few days before important birthdays within our families or our close friends. Imagine being able to remember everyone's birthdays without needing those calendar alerts! The Story Method can help you to do that, although again, it will take time to implant itself firmly and correctly in your mind.

If you have a lot of birthdays to remember, it might be a good idea to concentrate on a few select ones first of all. Go with the most important, perhaps your parents, your siblings, your partner and your best friend. Write them all down so you have information with which to form your story.

Start with the person who's birthday comes first in the year, so if you have a mother with a birthday in February, your father in June, your partner in August and your sister's birthday in October, you need to work in that order. Come up with a visually stimulating story which starts in February, linking your mother's birthday to your father's birthday in June, and so on. If you want to add dates in, you can do that too!

Practice your new story until it sticks in your mind and you're able to easily remember these key birthdays. Once that's firm in your memory, look to add a few new ones in and see how easily you can recall them.

Task 2 - Can You Remember Week 2's Chain Link Example?

In week 2 we introduced the Chain Link Method, as part of the overall Link Method. Can you remember the example we used then? To refresh your memory, we tried to remember your shopping list, using this particular chain linking strategy.

Without looking back over any notes you've made or refreshing your memory on the Chain Link Method at this point, you can remember

Points to Remember From This Chapter

In this chapter we have introduced the Link System, covering the Story Method and the Chain Link Method. These are similar systems but they're also very useful when trying to remember a larger amount of information. By using your imagination and letting the images in your mind run free, you can link together information which might have no literal connection in real life.

This helps you to keep a large amount of this knowledge in your memory bank, ready for recall whenever necessary.

The main points to take from this chapter are:

•	We use our imagination less as we grow up, but learning how to tap back into it will help you remember more

•	The Story Method is a great way to link together pieces of information which may have some slight connection to one another, by using your imagination to create a story

•	The Chain Link Method uses the same foundation as the Story Method, but it helps you to remember information which may have no sensical link. In this case, you would use your imagination to create a link, with the more obscure images being easier to remember.

Chapter 8: SMART Memory Course Part 4 - The Location Method (Loci)

Month 4! You're almost there, you're almost at the finishing point of completing the SMART Memory Course. This doesn't mean your memory is as good as it is ever going to be, of course; this is something which you need to continue using, otherwise you literally do lose it. In that case, keep using the techniques we've taught you throughout the course, and find ways which you find easy to help recall important information, whenever you need it.

In this month, our penultimate month, we're going to introduce the Location Method, sometimes referred to as Loci Method. This method encompasses two main strategies, namely the Roman Room Method and the Journey Method. Both of these methods use visualization and imagination, as many of our strategies so far also have. You might hear the Roman Room Method called Memory Palace Method, but it's important to realize that this is one and the same.

Week 1

This week we're going to introduce you to the Roman Room Method, or as we just mentioned, the Memory Palace. This is a method which requires you to use your imagination a great deal, but it's one which can help you to remember a lot of information, in a short amount of time. We're also going to explore why locations as a base are ideal for committing items to your memory bank.

Your tasks for this week are:

- Identify a favorite place as your location memory base
- Introduce the Roman Room Method

Task 1 - Identify a favorite place as your location memory base

Before we introduce the full Roman Room Method to you, we need to explore memory bases. The Location Method as a whole uses, as the name would suggest, locations as a base. This is somewhere you feel safe, somewhere you know, and somewhere you can imagine in your mind's eye, and set within it certain memory triggers, to help you remember various pieces of information.

Your first task for this week is to identify your personal location memory base. This can be an old house you know well, your old school classroom, perhaps somewhere you have worked in the past, or simply a room which you like, somewhere you've spent a lot of time and somewhere you can picture in your mind very clearly.

It helps if this room is somewhere you've spent time because you can feel the space, not just see it. That will help you to commit items to your memory far more effective and help with your visualization efforts.

So, choose somewhere which you're going to use as your personal location memory base from now one. As we introduce the two umbrella strategies within the Location Method niche, you're going to use this base and expand on it a little more. Spend some time exploring it in your mind, using your imagination and trying to imagine yourself back in that place, feeling its energy, it's temperature, how comfortable it is, etc. The clearer you can imagine it, the more effective it will be as your memory base.

Task 2 - Introduce the Roman Room Method

Within the Location Method as a whole there are two umbrella methods, as we have already mentioned. Your second task for this week is to learn about the Roman Room Method and use it for the first time. Remember, you might also hear this method called Memory Palace, so don't become confused between the two terms.

To use this method you need to go back to your memory location base, which you identified as your first task for this week. Before you begin, think about the items that are in that room. The reason you need to focus on the items is because they're going to be your memory markers for whatever it is you want to remember.

Let's imagine that you want to remember the world's big capital cities. We used this example before, so you can compare and contrast whether this is a better way to remember them or the Story Method we used earlier.

Picture your location memory base for a moment and think about the items that are within it. If you use your bedroom, there might be your bed, an arm chair, a set of drawers, a dressing table, a large window, a bookcase with many books, a carpet on the floor, etc. For each of those items you need to attach a capital city. So, your bed could have a duvet cover with the Eiffel Tower on it, symbolizing Paris. Your wall might have a picture of Real Madrid Football Club on it, symbolizing Madrid. You might have a red telephone box ornament on your dressing table, symbolizing London.

Once you've set capital cities to the items in your room, close your eyes and imagine yourself walking into your room and seeing those items. You'll really need to focus, especially if you're trying to remember many different pieces of information within that room.

Again, this is something you'll need to practice, but you can also use it to try and remember information in order. Some people use the Roman Room method to help them remember speeches, e.g. different subjects within that speech, in the order in which they walk into the room and see various different items.

This method is very useful and very effective, but it does rely upon really being able to visualize the room and the items you're using as markers. Again, practice will make perfect.

WEEK 2

The Roman Room method we talked about last week is something you should continue to practice as we move onto the second week of this month and beyond, but we're also going to introduce another strategy this week, called the Journey Technique.

Your tasks for this week are:

- Introduce the Journey Technique
- Perform a memory sweep - can you see an improvement?

Task 1 - Introduce the Journey Technique

In many ways, the Journey Technique sues a very similar method to the Roman Room Method, but it uses a journey rather than a specific room. This gives you a little more creative license.

Picture a journey that you know very well. It could be your commute to work, it could be a walk you take every weekend, or a hiking trail that you love. The idea is that you know this journey well enough to pull it to the front of your mind with ease and that you can picture the various milestones and landmarks you pass every single time you travel through it.

It's a good idea to sit down and write the journey out, making any specific points which stand out, such as a very pretty rosebush, a bridge, a busy road crossing, a patch of old trees, etc. You are going to attach various pieces of information you need to remember to each of these landmarks or points of interest, so make sure you're aware of them and that you can picture them very clearly in your mind as you take that journey.

Let's say you want to remember your shopping list, just as a quick and simple example. On your list you have tea, milk, bread, sugar, coffee, tomatoes, and lettuce.

You would picture the journey in your mind and imagine yourself walking or driving along, and for each landmark you would remember a piece of shopping you need to buy. Perhaps you walk past a picnic table in the park and there is a cup of tea on the bench, you carry and you see a cow in the opposite field, telling you that you need to buy milk. You carry on and you notice white square stones along the hedgerow, which look just like sugar cubes, etc.

The more imaginative your journey, the more you'll be able to remember but it also relies upon you being able to see real-time landmarks and items, to help you remember the items easily. It's no good imagining that there are chickens in the road if you live in the city and chickens are the last thing you would expect to see. It might be surreal enough to help you remember it once, but it's not going to help you remember it on a regular basis!

Give it a try and see how you find the Journey Method, before comparing it to the Roman Room Method. Which do you prefer?

Task 2 - Perform a memory sweep

We've given you two new strategies to try in the first two weeks of this month, so without wanting to overload you, your second task for this week is to look back over your progress and see if you've actually managed to improve any aspects of your memory so far.

We will call this a 'memory sweep'.

Think back to your starting point and then compare where you are now. What differences can you see?

It's important to do these check ins with yourself as they help you to measure results, whilst also motiving you to continue on with you efforts.

If you're not seeing the amount of improvement you would have hoped for, can you identify a reason as to why that is? Did you have unrealistic expectations? Have you been doing your homework throughout the week? Do you think you're perhaps not getting enough sleep?

Whilst you shouldn't expect miracles within four months, you should now be seeing some serious results coming your way. Make this week's second task the time you take a realistic look at how far you've come and evaluate whether it's enough for you, or not. If not, increase your efforts to get the results you want.

Week 3

You have learnt two new strategies this month; do you like one more than other? Is there one which you find easier naturally? It's quite likely that you either find the static exploration of the Roman Room or the movement of the Journey Method easier. Maybe you enjoy them both, but there's likely to be one which you naturally gravitate towards.

In this, our third week of our penultimate month, we're going to focus on recaps again. By this point you will understand the importance of revising areas we've introduced throughout the months - you don't learn something by doing it only once!

Your tasks for this week are:

- Recap on your imagination skills
- Identify your favorite technique so far

Task 1 - Recap on your imagination skills

Last month we tasked you with using your imagination more, and letting it run free when you're calm and relaxed. Your first task for this week is to continue with that strategy and perhaps see if you can identify any blocks to your imagination.

Do you find it easier to imagine animals rather than people? Do you find it easier to imagine places you've never been or places you have been? Is your imagination triggered by colorful situations or do you prefer natural settings? Everyone is different and it's likely that you have situations and elements which kickstart you imagination easier than others.

Understanding those triggers can help you to use your imagination more, and also allow you to create useful memory markers and images in your mind whenever you need to. If you find it easier to imagine animals than people, your most effective memory markers should revolve around the animal world, and you should leave people to someone else!

Spend a little more time working on using your imagination. If you find it hard to sit there and visualize things sometimes, perhaps because you're tired or stressed, why not work on writing a short story? This is another way to allow your imagination to run wild, as you're not only writing down the words, but you're creating a picture in your mind, therefore kickstarting your imagination very easily.

Give it go!

Task 2 - Identify your favorite technique so far

Whilst you're practicing your imagination skills, maybe even writing that short story we mentioned, have a think about which of the strategies we've talked about so far is your favorite. Which one do you find easiest to use?

The reason for exploring this as the second task for this week isn't simply so you can look back at your progress and pat yourself on the back (although you should certainly be doing that), but it's to help you identify if you're using one method more than the others.

The reason for showing you various different memory strategies isn't so you can choose your favorite and use that one all the time, it's so you can choose a specific strategy to fit a specific situation at the time. For that reason, throughout the SMART Memory Course, we're careful to introduce a new strategy, but also task you with revisiting an older one. You need to be able to use these strategies interchangeably. Whilst they might not all work for you, you should have a few which you can use whenever you need to.

So, which do you think you've naturally gravitated towards so far? Which have you struggled with? Identifying the answer to that particular question means you need to work towards improving your performance with your personal trouble-spot strategy. Perhaps you just need to practice a little more, or maybe you didn't quite grasp it the first time. If that's the reason, simply go back over and start from scratch - some techniques will click easier than others, but that doesn't mean they're a lost cause for you.

Week 4

You're almost at the end of month 4 and that means the final month of the SMART Memory Course is looming large! We have one last memory system to introduce to you in month 5, but at this point you have much of the knowledge you need; you simply need to use it and practice!

Your tasks for this week are:

- Revisit the Acronym Method
- Understand your memory blocks

The final week of this month is going to be about recapping and thinking a little deeper.

Task 1 - Revisit the Acronym Method

Back in month 2 we introduced to you the Acronym Method. This was a combination of two strategies, namely the Acronym Mnemonic Technique and the Sentence Method. Can you remember those now or do you need to head back and re-read? If that's the case, go for it!

Your first task this week is to revisit that method and use it to remember something different to when you first tried it. This can be either the mnemonic method or the sentence method, whichever works for you. By revisiting this method, you're refreshing your memory, but you're also giving it another try, to see which of the two strategies is your personal preference.

Do you find it easier to remember a word made up of the first letters of information you want to remember, or do you find it easier to remember a sentence, such as the famous 'Richard of York Gave Battle in Vain'?

Again, you're likely to have a natural preference, but that means you should try and use the other method a little more and work through any potential issues you have with it. By practicing both again, you're giving yourself the tools to identify that information.

Task 2 - Understand your memory blocks

Your final task of this month is to identify any potential memory blocks you have and then work to smash them with an imaginary sledge hammer!

Do you find that you're able to remember things more clearly in the morning versus the evening time? Do you find that your memory is more effective after a meal or before? Think carefully about your lifestyle routine and work out whether you have memory highs or lows at any stage.

Some might be quite obvious, e.g. you had a bad night's sleep so you find your memory and your brain in general are a little foggy the next day. That's normal and something which will pass, however if you notice that you have memory blocks at a certain time on a regular basis, you need to work towards overcoming them.

Start a memory diary once more and try and identify any problems you encounter throughout the days. You could keep this diary for a week or two and then look over your results and see what you can identify. Be sure to write down the time, what you were dong, what you did beforehand, and rate your memory power on a scale of 1 to 5, with 1 being poor and 5 being excellent.

By understanding your memory blocks, you can make changes and overcome problems which might have been holding you back without realizing it.

Points to Remember From This Chapter

This chapter has introduced the penultimate memory system we're going to cover, the Location Method, or Loci Method. Within this we've covered the Journey System and the Roman Room Method. Which do you prefer? Most people have a preference, but it's a good idea to try and master both.

The main points to take from this chapter are:

•   The Location Method is sometimes referred to as 'Loci'
•   The Roman Room Method uses a location memory base to explore and identify pieces of information you want to remember, by tagging memory markers
•   The Journey Technique covers a familiar journey, and you

use landmarks you regularly encounter as your memory markers

•	Both methods use the imagination and visualization to help pull certain pieces of information to mind

•	Whilst you might have one or two favorite memory methods so far, it's important not to gravitate towards using just one. You should have a range you can use whenever the situation calls for them.

Chapter 9: SMART Memory Course Part 5 - The PEG System

We're into our final month of the SMART Memory Course. That doesn't mean the hard work is over, as this month is going to give you quite a lot of homework!

The final system we need to introduce you to is called the PEG System.

The PEG System consists of several strategies and techniques which you can use to remember small details or a list of information. The system works by attaching 'pegs' or markers to certain things, such as numbers, letters, body parts, whatever works for you.

Throughout the last four weeks of the course we will introduce a different strategy for you to try, whilst also encouraging you to go back over some the older techniques and refresh your memory. We'll end the month with a total review of your progress, so you can see how far you've come and pat yourself on the back as a result!

WEEK 1

Your first week's task for this month is a theory-based one. In order to help you use the PEG system effectively, you need to understand it and know how it works. From there, we can introduce the strategies within it, one by one.

The PEG system can be numbers or letters, but you can use body parts as well if it works best for you. Despite that, we're going to focus on the letters and numbers for this month, as those are the predominant methods and the ones which will bring you the most benefit.

Your tasks for this week are:

- Introduce and overview the PEG System
- Use the Alphabet System

Task 1 - Introduce and overview the PEG System

Your first task for this week is to grasp the PEG System completely, before we move on to introducing the specific strategies next week and beyond. Understanding is vital if you want to truly learn how to use something properly, and whilst this system is very useful, it can be a little difficult to understand at the start.

Let's explain.

The PEG System is sometimes referred to as a mnemonic system, but it takes the theory a step further. Overall, if you need to remember information in a specific order, this system will work very well.

Using numbers or letters, you attach 'pegs' or pieces of information you want to remember to each one. For instance, if you were using letters you would attach 'apple' to A and you would picture an apple. Of course, it's a little more in-depth than that in theory, but it's a good way to show you a brief example.

You might hear the 'pegs' referred to as "mental hooks", but these are designed to hang information off of and then memorize it using visualization. Of course, you're used to using your imagination and your visualization skills now, so that shouldn't be a problem! If you find that you're still having problems remembering the images you attach to these pegs, you can do a little more imagination work by recapping on the exercise we used last month.

The theory goes that you already know the alphabet and you already know how to count, so you're not going to forget the information on which you're going to place hangers or 'pegs'. The information you put onto these will then be remember continually because you have that basic knowledge.

You might think in that case that you can only use this system in order to recall one set of information, but that's not the case. Many people use the PEG System several times over, using the numbers 1 to 10 to remember many different things, creating different sets of memory recall. The human brain is incredibly complex, so by visualizing different 'pegs' you can use this system time and time again.

However, at the start it is better to use different methods in order to remember information. So, you could use numbers for one set, letters for another, etc, until you start to build up your skills in this system.

This week's first task is therefore to understand the theory behind this particular system, and then we are going to move on to introducing the first strategy within it, the Alphabet System.

Task 2 - Use the Alphabet System

Now you have the theory of the PEG System in your mind, you're ready to get started with the first technique. To give you some bad news, we're going to start with the most complex of all the strategies we've introduced so far! Despite that, the Alphabet Technique is one of the most effective in terms of remembering a lot of information, e.g. 26 pieces of information, one for each letter of the alphabet.

The simplest way to explain the Alphabet System is this; you choose specific images which mean something to you and can be remembered easily and you attach them to the letters. You can either go with the first letter of the word and attach it to the specific letter, or you can go phonetically and opt for the first syllable, i.e. the sound it makes. In that case, you could attach the word 'seasoning' to C, because although it doesn't start with the letter C, it sounds like the letter phonetically.

Grab a piece of paper and write the letters A to Z down one side of the page, in a list. Then, choose a word to attach to each letter, opting for words which you can remember yourself. We could give you a list of suggestions, but it would be no use because everyone is different can remember different images, as per their personal preferences!

To give you the general feel of what you're aiming towards however, you could go with:

A - Apple
B - Bee
C - Car

The list would continue that way. If you wanted to go down the phonetic route, a strategy called the Letter Sound Method, you could go with:

A - Ant
B - Bean
C - Seasoning

Choose the method you think works best for you, but for beginners the first letter method is probably easier.

Once you've come up with an easy to recognise word for each

letter, spend some time memorizing it and trying to commit it to your memory bank. This is likely to take time, but once you've got it stuck in there, you'll be able to use it to remember large pieces of information (up to 26 pieces at any one time).

If you were then trying to remember a shopping list, such as milk, sugar, and bread, you could visualize the following:

A - Apple - Milk added apple to make a strange apple milkshake
B - Bee - Bees are attracted to honey which tastes sugary
C - Car - Bread with four wheels

You can take this as obscure as you like, but as with the other memory methods we've talked about so far, this method requires a large amount of visualization in order to make it work.

Your second task for this week is to understand the Alphabet System and come up with your own personal list of A to Z words. Once you've done that, use the system for the first time and continue to practice it as the weeks go on. If you struggle to remember your list at first, stick with it and keep trying to commit to to your mind. You could even use a mind map for this if you wanted to and combine two strategies in one!

WEEK 2

Last week's tasks were quite full on, and this week we're going to continue at the same rate, whilst encouraging you to revisit a method we introduced last month.

The Major System is part of the PEG System and whilst it might seem complicated at first, it's actually a very easy to use system once you get used to it. This week's first task it to understand the Major System and begin to use it.

Your tasks for this week are:

- Introduce the Major System and begin to use it
- Revisit the Journey Technique

Task 1 - Introduce and begin to use the Major System

The Major System is a very useful way to remember numbers. Despite that, you're not actually going to be using numbers when you attempt to remember them, you're actually going to turn the into letters and then into corresponding images. The reason is because images are thought to be far easier to remember than numbers.

You might sometimes hear this particular system called Herigone's Mnemonic System, the Phonetic Number System or the Phonetic Mnemonic System, but it's all one and the same. There has been a huge amount of change to this system over the years, but the current model is thought to be the easiest to remember.

To break it down to the most simplistic explanation, the Major System takes a number and then changes it into a sound (consonant letter) and then adds vowels to create a word. The letters added help you to create images which allow you to remember numbers over the long-term.

Again, it sounds complicated, so let's give an example and explain it a little more clearly.

0 is attached to the letters s, z and c
1 is attached to t and d
2 is attached to n
3 is attached to m
4 is attached to r
5 is attached to l
6 is attached to j, sh,ch, zh, and g
7 is attached to hard c and g, q, qu, and k
8 is attached to f and v
9 is attached to b and p

The reasons for attaching these letters to these numbers vary, but it's mainly because of how they look when flipped sideways or backwards and whether they have any connection to Roman numerals. It's not really useful to understand why, it's simply better to focus on memorizing the list and then looking at how you attach images to the words you create.

It's worth pointing out that when you create words from these letters, you shouldn't focus on the exact spelling and instead you should think about how they sounds, e.g. phonetic.

So, to create the letter combination 305, you could use the word 'missile'.

You would create this by taking 3 (m), 0 (s), and 5 (l). Then, add in vowels to create a word that makes sense. From that you could get 'missile' and you would add a visual image of a missile taking off to help it stick in your mind.

Of course, it doesn't have to be 'missile', it can be anything that you feel you're more likely to remember, by adding in vowels to create a word that makes sense to you.

If you wanted to remember a telephone numbers of 305701, you could create the words 'missile ghost' and create an image of those words which make sense to you. By doing that, you would take the 305 missile and you could great the word 'ghost' from the attached consonants of 701. By picturing a missile with a ghost on it, you will be able to remember this telephone number over the long term.

That is however just an example and you can create endless combinations of numbers, letters and then images by using the Major System. Despite that, it does take some work because you need to memorize and use the number and letter combinations before you can start to utilize it fully.

Your first task for this week is to understand the Major System, start memorizing the table of attached numbers and consonant sounds, and then try remembering one combination of numbers to see how you get on. Again, over the coming weeks make sure that you continue to use this system in order to practice your competency.

Task 2 - Revisit the Journey Technique

Over the last two weeks you have worked very hard on learning two quite difficult PEG System techniques. To give you a slight break for your second task this week, you are to go back over the Journey Technique from last month.

If you need a quick recap on what this technique is about, simply head back and go over it once more, but to summarize - you are to remember a journey you know well and then use markers (landmarks) to remember certain items. You practiced this method last month and tried it out and hopefully you will have continued to use it since then. Your second task for this week is to try and remember something different using this technique and see whether your performance the second time around is more successful than the first.

Week 3

You're almost there! Just two more weeks to go and you've finished the SMART Memory Course. This week we're going to introduce another of the PEG System strategies, namely the Number Shape Method.

Last week we introduced the Major System as a way to remember numbers as images, and this week we're taking it a step further. The difference between this system and the last one is that the images you attach to the numbers are based on how the number looks, e.g. if the number is round (0) you would attach an image which looks like a ball or another round object.

Your tasks for this week are:

- Introduce the Number Shape Method
- Review your memory block progress

Task 1 - Introduce the Number Shape Method

Remembering numbers can be tough and it might be that you simply don't find the Major System to be so useful for you. That's fine - not every system is going to work for you, but the good news is that remembering numbers can be done via the Number Shape Method too.

This method, as we just touched upon, works with the shape of the letter and what it reminds you of. For that reason, there is no set table of attached words or images to memorize, it completely comes down to your imagination and what the letters represent to you.

A few suggestions might include:

0 - beach ball
1 - stick
2 - shark
3 - butterfly
4 - flag
5 - Superman
6 - cherry
7 - axe
8 - hourglass
9 - balloon

These are just suggestions, and it's important to go with an image that sticks in your mind and really fires your imagination. Take sometime working out which images work for you, and write down your own personal list. This list is going to be your go-to for remembering number combination and from those words you're going to create images.

So, assuming you were going to work with the list above and you wanted to remember the numbers 249, you could imagine a shark eating a flag with a balloon stuck to it.

It can be as strange and as obscure as you want it to be, as long as it makes sense to you! You can even learn telephone numbers this way. For example, 524376 could be:

5 - Superman
2 - shark
4 - flag
3 - butterfly
7 - axe
6 - cherry

Superman could be chasing a shark, but he sees a flag with a butterfly on it. Suddenly an axe is thrown his way and he catches it, and sees a cherry attached to the handle.

Again, completely obscure, but if you can remember it, and remember the numbers in the right order, you'll never forget this telephone number!

Your first task for this week is to work out which images you would like to attach to each of the numbers, according to how they look to you. Perhaps you don't see an axe when you visualize the number 7, and maybe you see a boomerang instead. In that case, go with the boomerang! It has to be personal to you in order for you to remember it.

Once you've come up with your list, try and remember a series of numbers using your list and see how you go. Again, practice this method over the coming weeks.

Task 2 - Review your memory block progress

Last month we talked about memory blocks and how there are certain situations which might cause you to have a memory black out. Perhaps first thing the morning your memory is just not firing on all cylinders. One of your tasks from last week was to identify any blocks you have and to try and put measures into place to reduce their effect.

Your second task for this week is to review your progress and see if those measures you used have worked or not.

It's useful to look back over things like this, as you can't be sure if what you're doing is working unless you review it regularly. Maybe you made a change last month and you've noticed a small improvement. In that case, could you maximize this change and therefore improve even more?

Whatever changes you made, if you made any at all, work out how much of an effect they have had and then see if you can push it a little further still.

Week 4

Your final week is here! We have one more technique to show you and then we're going to do a full review and round up of your progress. Of course, that includes celebrating what you've learnt and how far you've come.

The final strategy is called the Number Rhyme Method and it's another method within the PEG System. As you will have noticed throughout this final month, the PEG System is a little more in-depth compared to some of the others we've covered so far. It's not that they're considered harder per-se, but they do require more imagination and in some cases, memorizing lists of information as a base.

Your tasks for this week are:

- Introduce the Number Rhyme Method
- Review your entire journey

Task 1 - Introduce the Number Rhyme Method

The good news is that the Number Rhyme Method is the easiest of the PEG system techniques. It also uses a high amount of visualization, creating stories to help you remember large amounts of information. This can help you to remember long numbers, such as telephone numbers by turning them into easier to remember images.

The Number Rhyme Method is another of the mnemonic methods, and the image you attach to the number is a word which rhymes with the number. For instance, 1 rhymes with sun, so you would attach a sun to the number 1.

A few other suggestions include:

0 - hero (zero rhymes with hero)
1 - sun
2 - glue
3 - bee
4 - boar
5 - jive
6 - kicks
7 - heaven
8 - gate
9 - wine

You can use this list of numbers and associated images to remember long number combinations or you can also use them to remember lists of items, such as a shopping list, by turning them back into numbers. It all hinges on you remembering the pegs you've attached to each of the numbers, e.g. wine will always remind you of number 9.

Let's say you wanted to remember the number combination 207598. The images would be:

glue, hero, heaven, jive, wine, and gate.

So, how can you remember that number combination from these images? You create a story, that's how! It can be whatever you want it to be, but perhaps it could a little like this example:

There is patch of glue on the floor and the hero of the hour has flown down from heaven and become stuck in it. He tries to do a little jive movement to get away but it's not working. He read somewhere that pouring wine onto glue might help him become unstuck, but the last time he tried that he remained stuck to the gate.

Again, it's random, but if you can remember the story and the associated numbers for the pegs, you'll always remember that combination of letters.

You can also flip this around and remember a list of images too. It doesn't always have to be numbers although this method is predominantly associated with numbers first and foremost.

Your first task for this, our final week, is to come up with your own personal list of images for each of the numbers, according to the sound of the number what it rhymes with to your own ears. Memorize it and see how quick you can commit it to your memory, compared with the first few techniques you tried to memorize at the start of the course. Do you notice an improvement in how quickly you can keep things in your memory bank?

From there, try remembering a few different number combination throughout the week and assess your progress.

Task 2 - Review your entire journey

On the final day of your last week of the SMART Memory Course, you need to sit down and assess your overall progress.

You've come a long way and you've learnt a lot, that's for sure!

We've walked you through several of the most popular and most successful memory improvement strategies, and you're sure to have a few favorites by this point.

The main aim of this review of your entire memory improvement journey is to see how far you've come, but also to open your eyes to what you've achieved and what your brain is actually capable of. Did you ever imagine you would get to the end of these five months, or did you think you would give up halfway through? Well done for sticking with it, and you'll see progress and improvement as a result.

As part of your last task, sit down and ask yourself these questions:

•   Can you see an improvement from day one to the final day of the SMART Memory Course?

•   What is your favorite memory improvement technique and why?

•   Which of the techniques have you found hardest to grasp?

•   Is there one specific technique which you really don't like? If so, why?

•   Do you find it easier to remember words or numbers?

•   Do you feel healthier as a result of changes to your lifestyle made at the start?

•   Do you think there are any other lifestyle changes you could make at this point?

•   Which of the techniques do you think you need to work on a little more?

Asking yourself these questions isn't just a quick survey and a pat on the back, although you should certainly be giving yourself that very firm pat on the back right now, it's also to help you identify where extra work might need to be done.

Remember, the journey isn't over just because we've come to the end of giving you weekly tasks to complete! The structure of this course is designed to drip-feed you new techniques on a regular basis, but as we've mentioned several times throughout, you need to focus on practicing them on a regular basis, otherwise they're not going to be any use to you.

Practice really does make perfect and when it comes to anything brain-related, it all comes down to repetition. The more you repeat something, the more familiar it becomes to you over time, forming new connections in your brain.

Of course, as we've now reached the final task of the SMART Memory Course, you should find a way to celebrate your progress.

Is there a reward you've been saving? If so, you can grab it now, you've done a lot of hard work and you deserve it! If you haven't been saving a reward, now is the time to think of one!

Points to Remember From This Chapter

Continuing to practice the various different methods we've covered throughout the course is vital. You cannot just practice them two or three times and then expect them to work for you, you need to keep working with them, in order to allow them to work for you.

This chapter has introduced the final memory improvement system, the PEG System. This has been quite a long chapter, all down to the fact that the PEG System is without a doubt the most complicated of all the systems we've covered so far. Yes, we saved the best for last!

Working through each of the strategies within this system one by one and slowly is the only way to work out which are ideal for you and which you might prefer not to work with quite so much in the future. Despite that, giving them all a try is a must do!

The main points to remember from this chapter are:

- Images are easier to remember than numbers
- The PEG System attaches pegs to something you already know, such as numbers or letters, and therefore helps you to remember larger pieces of information
- The Major System is certainly the most complicated of all

the PEG System techniques and requires some prior knowledge of the consonant sounds to be attached to specific numbers

•	We base information on numbers and letters because these are foundations we know well and which we are not going to forget.

Conclusion

And there we have it! You've done it, you've reached the end of five months of memory improvement and by now you should be able to remember far more, far easily, and for far longer!

How do you feel now? Do you feel more confident in your ability to keep things in your mind?

It's vital that you give yourself a huge pat on the back at this point and remind yourself of how far you've come. Despite that, the hard work isn't over; you need to continue practicing and trying to improve your performance.

This will certainly not be hard work done in vain!

By now you will certainly understand that despite the complexities of the human brain, it is an organ which can be manipulated to a certain degree. Researchers and scientists might still be trying to work out the inner mechanisms and how they relate to each other and perhaps we might never truly understand the brain's capacity in terms of performance and what it can really do, but we know that we can trick it into remember more!

This is extremely useful in many different aspects of your life. Not only does having a better memory help you become a more productive person, ensuring that you don't forget important details, but it also boosts your confidence in general and helps you to achieve more over the course of your work, your personal life, and in the goals you set for yourself.

You may never know your true memory potential, but over these last five months you've certainly tapped into what it's capable of. As you continue practicing and learning, you'll discover even more.

References &
Further Reading

1. Baddeley, A. D., Eysenck, M. W., & Anderson, M. C. (2015). Memory.

2. Buzan, T. (2007). Master your memory. Essex, BBC Active.

3. Buzan, T. (1991). Use your perfect memory. New York, N.Y., U.S.A., Plume Book.

4. Lillios, K. T., & Tsamis, V. (2010). Material mnemonics: Everyday memory in prehistoric Europe. Oxford: Oxbow Books.

5. Lorayne, H., & Lucas, J. (2017). The memory book: The classic guide to improving your memory at work, at school, and at play.

6. Schacter, D. L., & Tulving, E. (1994). Memory systems 1994. Cambridge, Mass: MIT Press.

7. Thompson, R. F., & Madigan, S. A. (2005). Memory: The key to consciousness. Washington, D.C: Joseph Henry Press.

8. Turkington, C. (1996). 12 steps to a better memory. New York: Macmillan USA.

9. Roediger, H. L., Dudai, Y., & Fitzpatrick, S. M. (2007). Science of memory: Concepts. Oxford: Oxford University Press.

10. Klingberg, T. (2009). The overflowing brain: Information overload and the limits of working memory. Oxford: Oxford University Press.

11. Royalty-free images from www.freepik.com.